MW01628679

JOSEPH HOLSTON

Color in Freedom

Journey Along the Underground Railroad

BARBARA STEPHANIC

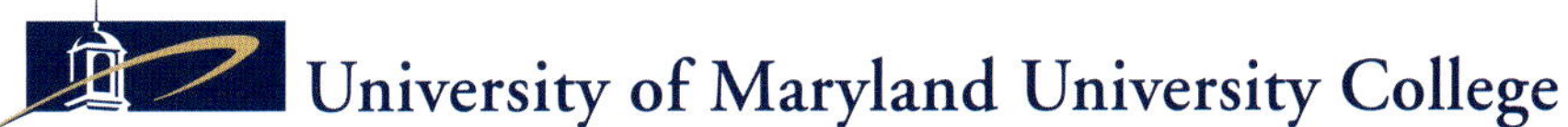

Pomegranate
SAN FRANCISCO

Published by Pomegranate Communications, Inc.
Box 808022, Petaluma CA 94975
800 227 1428   707 782 9000
www.pomegranate.com

Pomegranate Europe Ltd.
Unit 1, Heathcote Business Centre, Hurlbutt Road
Warwick, Warwickshire CV34 6TD, UK
[+44] 0 1926 430111
sales@pomeurope.co.uk

Front cover: *Sun Warms the Freemen,* 2008
Back cover: *Righteous Rejoicing,* 2008

Library of Congress Cataloging-in-Publication Data
Stephanic, Barbara.
Joseph Holston : color in freedom / Barbara Stephanic.
p. cm.
Includes bibliographical references.
ISBN 978-0-7649-4646-2 (hardcover)
1. Holston, Joseph, 1944- 2. Slavery in art. 3. African Americans in art. 4. Color in art. I. Title.
ND237.H6699S74 2008
759.13—dc22

2008009904

Pomegranate Catalog No. A154
Design by Lynn Bell, Monroe Street Studios, Santa Rosa, California

Printed in China
17 16 15 14 13 12 11 10 09 08   10 9 8 7 6 5 4 3 2 1

Contents

This art is dedicated to all—slave and free—

who lived, struggled, fought, and died

to paint the stories of their lives in

the magnificent colors of freedom.

—Joseph Holston

THE UNDERGROUND RAILROAD

Redrawing Understanding

Despite Lincoln's Emancipation Proclamation, Archer Alexander was still enslaved in Missouri in 1863. By that time, he had been held captive for more than thirty-five years. During the Civil War, Alexander secretly kept Union forces informed of the guerrilla activities of his pro-slavery, Southern-sympathizing enslaver until coming under suspicion as a "traitor." Rather than trust the outcome of an examination committee in Missouri, Alexander decided to escape. With no thought of assistance, without money, unarmed and in momentary danger of being killed, afraid to speak even to his wife, Alexander risked his life for the sake of liberty. The start of the Civil War had neither ensured his liberation nor eliminated the need or the quest for freedom. As martial law extended over the State of Missouri, placing anyone attempting to escape captivity under protection of the military authorities, Alexander became one of the last "fugitive slaves" captured in the state.[1] The Emancipation Proclamation of 1863 did not unilaterally grant freedom to all those held in slavery in the United States. It freed only those captives held in the rebelling states, and Missouri, although it had entered the Union as a slave state, fought for the Union.

Abolitionist William Greenleaf Eliot managed to secure Alexander's release from jail, but not his freedom—after which time Alexander paid a German farmer twenty dollars to bring his wife, Louisa, and children out of slavery. Keeping his word, the farmer loaded his ox-team wagon with corn shucks, loosely piling stalks under which Alexander's wife and thirteen-year-old daughter would hide. The farmer covered them with skillful carelessness, ensuring breathing space and concealment. He then drove on in the moonlit night, leisurely walking beside the oxen. After about a mile, the farmer was overtaken and asked whether he had seen two runaways, "a woman and a gal," anywhere on the road. "He stopped his team a minute, so as 'to talk polite,' and said, 'Yes, I saw them at the crossing, as I came along, standing, and looking scared-like, as if they were waiting for somebody; *but I have not seen them since.*' Literal truth is sometimes the most ingenious falsehood." The family joined Alexander in St. Louis in 1864—one year before all those enslaved in Missouri were manumitted, on January 11, 1865.[2]

Archer Alexander's story contains both exceptional and traditional components of the Underground Railroad narrative. Initially he escaped alone, but from Missouri rather than from the Deep South. The timing of his escape near the end of the Civil War, rather than in the 1830s or 1850s, places his quest for freedom outside Underground Railroad activities as they are conventionally understood. Alexander's story comes at the end of a historical period marked by the constant, centuries-long search for freedom.[3] Escape from captivity became the first, the most persistent, and the most consistent form of resistance to enslavement.[4]

Over the years, definitions of the Underground Railroad have been enigmatic, reflecting personal, local, and regional differences that formed and sustained its existence. Black abolitionist William Still, chairman and corresponding secretary for the Pennsylvania Vigilance Committee, chronicled his personal reminiscences and experiences relating to the Underground Railroad. Taking a modern-day ethnographic approach, Still collected and compiled the narratives of escapees fleeing mainly from Maryland, Delaware, Virginia, and the upper South as they passed through the Pennsylvania offices. Enamored with the language of the literal railroad, those involved with the figurative one used signals reflecting the latest, newest technology, and these became the hallmark of the Underground Railroad movement. Still imparted his firsthand knowledge of freedom seekers and the "conductors" and "stationmasters" who aided them.

The beginning of the classic period of the Underground Railroad has commonly centered on William Lloyd Garrison and his publication of *The Liberator* in 1831, extending through the start of the Civil War. Modern definitions, driven in part by the National Park Service's Network to Freedom initiative, expand the Underground Railroad beyond space and time to concept and metaphor, yielding a geographically and temporally unbounded redefinition that moves beyond the historically narrow slice of time between the emergence of *The Liberator* and the thunderous opening of the War of the Rebellion. The intervening thirty-year period became synonymous with the Underground Railroad, Quakers, and assisted escapes.

The Underground Railroad as remembered through this exhibition—at once myth, metaphor, and fact—elongates the time span and transcends locality to highlight escape from slavery whenever and wherever it occurred. No longer focused on Quakers, white abolitionists, and their aid to poor, shivering, frightened fugitives, this exhibition signals that we choose to remember the Underground Railroad as a phase along a continuum of escape—escape that began with the landing of the first slave ships and continued even after 1865, as people arrested for escaping or helping others to do so languished in jail after the war.[5]

The expanse of the Underground Railroad was for years limited in the American imagination, with each region of the country, each destination at the end of an escape route, imaging itself unique and preeminent. Levi Coffin glorified Indiana and Cincinnati, Wilbur Siebert shined his light first on

Ohio abolitionists, and William Still elevated Philadelphia, each shaping national awareness in regionally and locally particular, yet incomplete, ways. Through the Underground Railroad, each region had a different part to play in confronting the injustices of both slavery and the law. River towns, border states, and communities of free blacks functioned differently from northern urban centers in New England or along the Canada–US border. Only their purpose was the same: to provide a refuge from slavery or a conduit to freedom. "It is clear," note John Hope Franklin and Loren Schweninger in *Runaway Slaves: Rebels on the Plantation,* "some runaways had a network of Black friends and loved ones from whom they could expect assistance."[6]

Shifting focus away from the thirty-year classic period of the Underground Railroad as primary means of escape, Holston's exhibition considers the more than two centuries of escape tactics contained in an arsenal of freedom strategies as the enslaved made a way out of no way. The Underground Railroad was literally the end of a long line; the era was the last stop along the continuum of self-emancipation.

Escape was the first response to slavery throughout the African diaspora. In July of 1640, John Punch was captured in Maryland and returned to slavery in Virginia "for the time of his natural life." That same month and year, Emanuel received a whipping for the same offense. After receiving thirty lashes, he was ordered burned in the cheek with the letter *R*, literally a searing reminder of his attempted escape.[7]

By the early 1700s, slaveholders were trying to recover escaped captives by placing runaway slave advertisements in local newspapers. From these ads we learn about the brutality of slavery and about the advance planning on the part of the escapees, who often took a change of clothes, food, horses, money, and whatever else they thought might help in their flight to freedom. Many knew the secret of following the North Star; many knew the secret codes of literacy. Their narratives tell stories of escape through the eyes of the freedom seekers.

Persistent and long-term effects of escape from slavery can also be seen in the laws of the United States. Between the start of the American Revolution and the first constitutional Fugitive Slave Act of 1793, no fewer than eight fugitive clauses were included in various treaties in an attempt to control runaways. In 1785 the fugitive clause in King's ordinance stated that any escaped person "from whom labor or service is lawfully claimed in any one of the thirteen original States, such fugitive might be lawfully reclaimed and carried back to the person" enslaving him or her. So relentless were African captives in making their way out of slavery that between the foundation of the Constitution in 1778 and the opening salvo of the Civil War in 1861, no fewer than thirty-eight national acts, propositions, bills, and Indian treaties were enacted relative to escape from and control of slavery. The most notorious of these was the Fugitive Slave Act of 1850, which spurred the Underground Railroad movement and abolitionists, black and white, to new heights of defiance in opposition to the law.[8]

Long before the classic period of the Underground Railroad began in the 1830s, flight from slavery, Franklin and Schweninger emphasize, was the single most common act of slave resistance, aside from day-to-day defiance, which included withholding work, disobeying orders, or feigning illness. Over time, the character of escape shifted from solitary departures by men to include more groups and families attempting to free themselves from bondage. Individual escapes, such as those undertaken by J. C. Pennington or Harriet Tubman, were transformed during the traditional Underground Railroad period.[9] Slave narratives tell the stories of escape through the eyes of the freedom seeker. Unassisted individual and group escapes as recounted in the popular nineteenth- and early-twentieth-century narratives provide evidence and valuable descriptions that go beyond what is revealed in the self-proclaimed Underground Railroad genre written by operatives and conductors.

By 1840 free blacks living in stable rural communities at critical intersections along the border states, in urban centers, and in alleyways formed activist black institutions such as black churches, schools, and Masonic halls.[10] Abolitionists were also at the height of their activities during this period, many of whom were ready to offer assistance and encouragement to all who would take the risk of freedom. Known as the Underground Railroad, a systematic, interracial, cooperative method of aiding escaping slaves developed out of these combined forces.[11]

Rather than abandoning their country and fleeing to the foreign soil of Canada, Mexico, England, or the Caribbean—a tactic that escalated in the wake of the Fugitive Slave Act of 1850—escapees frequently took their chances, defying the law and remaining in one of the free states, seeking refuge and anonymity. The Underground Railroad histories of Boston, Syracuse, Buffalo, Philadelphia, Baltimore, Cincinnati, Detroit, Chicago, and a host of other major US cities reveal within the urban landscape communities and individuals of action.

Franklin and Schweninger estimate that by 1860 at least fifty thousand captives across the entire South were escaping annually.[12] Many of those seeking freedom ascribed their first undying resolution to strike for liberty to fear of the auction block, which frequently meant separation from loved ones.[13] Fears of impending sale, of kidnapping, of merciless brutality were among the multitude of factors that could trigger flight. Those pushed to such action often used waterways, mountain passes, caves, and other landscape features. A large majority of those who departed were young adult males, aged fifteen to thirty; disproportionate numbers of them lived or worked in urban areas and possessed craft or other marketable skills. These young, single males generally had fewer ties to the region they left, and their skills gave them a greater chance of succeeding economically.

Unlike the solitary escapes undertaken by men, women usually escaped in pairs or groups, particularly family groups, although there were numerous instances of individual escapes by women. Women frequently received outside assistance; they escaped with their husbands or with male relatives. On Harriet Tubman's first aborted escape attempt, she fled with her two brothers; after abandoning this effort, she later accomplished her mission alone after white neighbors gave her two names as well as instructions for finding her way to a house where she would receive aid. There she was placed in a wagon, covered with a sack, and smuggled to her next destination. She continued to receive and follow directions along the route to Pennsylvania, where she initially settled in Philadelphia. Tubman met Philadelphia stationmaster William Still, and with his invaluable assistance and that of other members of the Philadelphia Anti-Slavery Society, she learned the secrets of the Underground Railroad. "Traveling by night, hiding by day, scaling the mountains, fording the rivers, treading the forests, lying concealed as pursuers passed," turning south though journeying north, Tubman exploited the landscape as had so many escapees before her. One of her first rescue journeys took her to Baltimore to lead a female relative and her family out of slavery.[14]

Harriet Tubman endures as the greatest icon of the classic Underground Railroad period. Her efforts are most instructive. As with Tubman, concern for family was foremost on the minds of escapees, both women and men. Tubman's first "solemn resolution" upon leaving her home and family and escaping from slavery on the eastern shore of Maryland was that they, too, should be free. Her quest was to deliver her family from bondage and see them comfortably settled in the North. Indeed, on one of her last rescues on the Underground Railroad, in 1857, this ingenious woman fitted an old horse with a straw collar, rigged a footboard and a sitting board to an axle, and attached a pair of old chaise wheels to bring her seventy-year-old parents out of Maryland. Tubman returned to the eastern shore in an unsuccessful bid to rescue her sister and her sister's two children. Out of that failed venture, she did manage to help a group of thirty-nine escape. For all of her triumphs, however, Tubman's sister would die in slavery, and her children, Angerine and Ben, would remain enslaved despite Tubman spending a total of ten years attempting their rescue.[15]

Several of the incidents involving free blacks who were convicted of helping family members flee bondage would not have been counted among Underground Railroad escapes because many freedom seekers remained in the South in close proximity to family and loved ones. Concern for family was uppermost on the minds of women as well as men who escaped slavery, and escapees used various schemes and plans to free groups of people. The story of Margaret Garner, who, along with seventeen other people, seven of whom were her family members, attempted escape from a Kentucky plantation, stands out as one of the most dramatic. Paralleling the experience of so many others seeking freedom, the group was able to escape across the frozen Ohio River in the winter of 1856. As the escape plan collapsed, however, the family was left trapped and under siege by pursuers outside Cincinnati. Margaret Garner declared that she would kill herself and her four children before she would return to slavery. Seizing a butcher knife, with one stroke she cut the throat of her beloved little daughter Mary, from ear to ear, nearly severing the head from the body. Garner then tried to take the lives of her other three children as well as her own. Wholly bent on keeping her children out of slavery, and wielding a heavy coal shovel, she succeeded in smashing the face of her three-year-old daughter, Cilla. "Before she could complete her desperate work," the Garners, after fighting "with the ferocity of tigers," were overpowered by an armed posse of eleven slave catchers who had pursued the family and surrounded the house of a black relative in Cincinnati where they had taken refuge. Although the Garner tragedy is extreme among Underground Railroad narratives, the story exposes the wounds of slavery and the extent of African American determination to escape.[16]

That determination extended across the long expanse of slavery in the United States, from its earliest moments in Virginia to the closing days of the Civil War. From the American Revolution, when blacks first began to escape in large numbers, to the contrabands seeking refuge with the Union Army, the chaos and confusion of war provided self-liberators another opportunity to exploit in their quest for freedom. Blacks fought in the military as well, siding with whoever seemed most likely to grant the freedom and liberty the country espoused. They fought for liberty first with the British or the Continental Army during the American Revolution, and later with the United States Colored Troops during the Civil War, marking the culmination of centuries of efforts to end slavery.

Which brings us back to Archer Alexander.[17] His son Thomas had enlisted in the Union Army and fought on the battlefield. He was among the first black recruits and was killed in a brave charge by the Colored Troops at Hilton Head. Alexander's son would be one among more than two hundred thousand former slaves and freedmen who saw the Civil War as one more opportunity to ensure freedom by fighting to bring slavery to an end.

The Underground Railroad dwells in the national imagination as a well-known yet poorly understood icon. Over the years, white abolitionism has dominated the shape and scope of the Underground Railroad narrative, leaving the liberation strategies of African captives and freedmen and freedwomen a distant consideration. The story of blacks ensuring their own liberation in the midst of constant economic, social, judicial, and educational hardships brings a new dimension to our understanding. Focusing on the early history of black men and women working together, with or without abolitionists, across the United States and into Canada reveals an Underground Railroad quite different from the episodic, static, and individual-hero-driven narrative now enshrined in the popular imagination.

—*Cheryl Janifer LaRoche, PhD*

Notes

1. John W. Blassingame, ed., *Slave Testimony: Two Centuries of Letters, Speeches, Interviews, and Autobiographies* (Baton Rouge: Louisiana State University Press, 1977).

2. William G. Eliot, *The Story of Archer Alexander: From Slavery to Freedom, March 30, 1863* (Boston: Cupples, Upham and Company, 1885; University Library, University of North Carolina at Chapel Hill, 1999), 47, http://docsouth.unc.edu/neh/eliot/eliot.html.

3. Blassingame, *Slave Testimony,* 222.

4. Ibid.

5. Baltimore City and County Jail (Runaway Docket), #1268, Maryland State Archives C 2064-2, Maryland State House nomination; Secretary of State (Pardon Papers), 1851, Box 48, Folder 28, Maryland State Archives S 1031–10.

6. John Hope Franklin and Loren Schweninger, *Runaway Slaves: Rebels on the Plantation* (New York: Oxford University Press, 1999), 68.

7. Helen Tunnicliff Catterall, ed., *Judicial Cases Concerning American Slavery and the Negro,* Vol. I (Washington, DC: Carnegie Institution of Washington, 1926; New York: Octagon Books, 1968), 77.

8. Marion Gleason McDougall, *Fugitive Slaves, 1619–1865* (Boston: Ginn & Company, 1891; New York: Bergman Publishers, 1969).

9. J. C. Pennington, "The Fugitive Blacksmith; or, Events in the History of James W. C. Pennington, Pastor of a Presbyterian Church, New York, Formerly a Slave in the State of Maryland," in Arna Bontemps, *Great Slave Narratives* (Boston: Beacon Press, 1969). Born into slavery in Maryland in 1809, James William Charles Pennington, a proud and skilled blacksmith, escaped slavery after the "deep insult" of witnessing the whipping of his father. Pennington declared, ". . . in my mind and spirit, I was never a *Slave* after it." After receiving his own brutal beating at the hand of the Maryland slaveholder, Pennington embarked on his unforgettable journey of escape to Pennsylvania while in his early twenties. Pennington later became a Presbyterian minister and a black abolitionist noted for marrying Frederick Bailey (Douglass) to Anna Murray in New York City after Douglass escaped from Baltimore in 1838.

10. Cheryl J. LaRoche, "On the Edge of Freedom: Free Black Communities, Archaeology, and the Underground Railroad" (PhD diss., University of Maryland, 2004).

11. Joseph Cephas Carroll, *Slave Insurrections in the United States, 1800–1865* (Mineola, NY: Dover, 2004), 182; Wilbur H. Siebert, *The Underground Railroad from Slavery to Freedom* (New York: Macmillan, 1898), 25; Ann Hagedorn, *Beyond the River: The Untold Story of the Heroes of the Underground Railroad* (New York: Simon and Schuster, 2002).

12. Franklin and Schweninger, *Runaway Slaves,* 279–282.

13. William Still, *The Underground Railroad* (Philadelphia: Porter & Coates, 1872).

14. Kate Clifford Larson, *Harriet Tubman: Portrait of an American Hero* (New York: Ballantine Books, 2004); Earl Conrad, *Harriet Tubman: Negro Soldier and Abolitionist* (New York: International Publishers Co., 1942), 57; Sarah H. Bradford, *Harriet Tubman: The Moses of Her People* (Bedford, MA: Applewood Books, 1886), 30–31; Franklin and Schweninger, *Runaway Slaves,* 124–148.

15. Larson, *Harriet Tubman,* cited in Cheryl Janifer LaRoche, "Coerced But Not Subdued: Gendered Resistance of Women Escaping Slavery," in *Gendered Resistance,* ed. Mary Frederickson and Delores Walters. Manuscript on file with the author.

16. Steven Weisenburger, *Modern Medea: A Family Story of Slavery and Child-Murder from the Old South* (New York: Hill and Wang, 1998), 72–75; Levi Coffin, *Reminiscences of Levi Coffin, the Reputed President of the Underground Railroad* (Cincinnati: Western Tract Society, 1876), 557–561.

17. The likeness of Alexander is preserved in the Freedmen's Memorial Monument to Abraham Lincoln. Sculptor Thomas Ball modeled the face of the kneeling freedman from a photograph of Alexander. The statue stands in Lincoln Park in southeastern Washington, DC. See Kirk Savage, *Standing Soldiers, Kneeling Slaves: Race, War, and Monument in Nineteenth-Century America* (Princeton: Princeton University Press, 1997), 115.

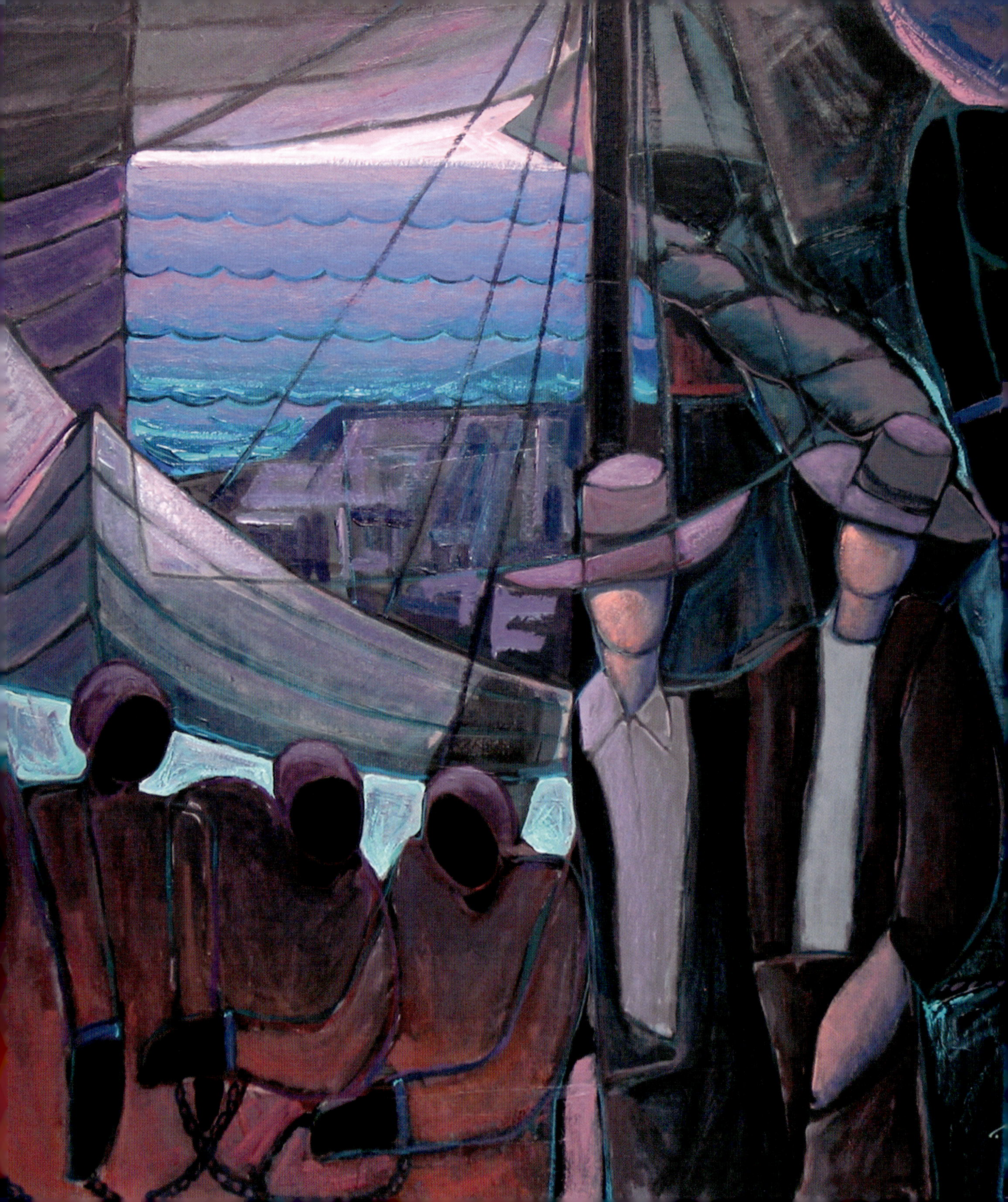

COLOR IN FREEDOM

Journey Along the Underground Railroad

Why should I be a slave?

There was no reason why I should be the thrall of any man.

FREDERICK DOUGLASS[1]

This exhibition will lead viewers along a historic path that marks the quest for freedom in America. Its works are divided into four distinct segments, the divisions analogous to the movements in a musical score. In it, Joseph Holston chronicles slavery in America through artistic interpretation, presenting a body of work that reads like an epic poem—one moving in a steady, continuing rhythm through this period in American history. He expresses his heartfelt feelings in successive rhythmic movements that flow through each exhibition segment. Within this harmonious theme, he remains sensitive to those courageous men and women who were subjected to bondage and to those who made a heroic escape. Here in this discussion of his work, their voices—some well known, others less familiar—are heard recounting personal reminiscences and individual experiences.

Throughout the visual journey this exhibition presents, Holston remains optimistic for the future of those whose lives it celebrates. Even when portraying the darkest hours, he illuminates each composition with light rendered in the subtlest shades of soft, warm tones or in the boldest, most vibrant colors, the effects suggesting hope and possibility. The luminosity of Holston's palette produces a radiance of color, with palpable rather than fluid brush strokes. The light appears radiant and painterly, leaving the viewer with an illusion of atmosphere and air circulating around the canvas. The minute tonal modulations mimic the effect of a glowing illumination penetrating the darkness.

The paintings are organized in a linear chronology that is at once musical and pictorial. Each of the four "movements" of the exhibition is faithful to a particular period of slavery in America: first, the arrival in an unknown world; second, the adjustment to living in bondage among

Left: *Arrival in the Unknown* (detail)

strangers; third, the personal journey of escape; and fourth, the glory of freedom. Holston's account of the complex passage is expressed in a symphony of relationships between light, color, and form set to a musical sense of time and perception. His compositions create a "fugue in colors," evoking motifs in a kinetic rhythm that moves the viewer along this historic path.

Musicians and painters share many creative ideas as well as the terms used to express them. They have often, throughout history, played harmonious duets together. Both the painter and the composer are concerned with composition; both consider tone—a color value for one and an audio quality for the other. Rhythmic pattern is seen in the repetition of color and form in a painting just as it is heard in the melody of a symphony. Artists often consider the tempo of pattern change as a means to express intensity and reference unity, just as a musician will set the tempo to increase or decrease intensity of sound. Both painting and music are equally capable of stimulating passion; they can convey the greatest delight as well as a sense of sorrow.[2]

Viewing the work in this exhibition with the musical theme in mind is relevant, both because of the artist's inspired connection with music and for the effects of music on the human spirit. Holston is an artist for whom music is a key source of innovation. He is part of a long tradition of artists whose muse is music and its relationship to painting. Abstract painters have for decades been intrigued by the freedom of line and form, rejecting the literal imitation of nature. Similarly, a feeling of sovereign independence reverberates from musical scores whose tonal harmony is derived from intrinsic means. Holston shows us how elements of painting are composed in a similar way to musical scores, and how repetitive shapes and forms can bring rhythm to a visual composition just as a sequence of musical notes can to a song. The connecting transition from one sound to another can express a spiritual harmony in the same way that colors can produce a resonance that evokes an emotional response. In this way the vast array of emotions brought forth by convoluted layers of paint reverberates almost audibly off the canvas.

Music can be a powerful influence on the painter's vision and can shape the communication of a personal view, a poignant idea, or an impassioned mood. This is important to remember in the context of Holston's work, given his admitted inspiration from music and the emotion it evokes. Yet the reference to music is relevant for another reason as well: Consider the power and significance of music to the African men and women who brought their euphonic traditions to the American continent. Given the diversity among the first generation of the enslaved population—their different cultural traditions, customs, belief systems, and languages—it was often music that provided a common means of communication. Music, singing, and dancing were as much a part of the African culture as the oral tradition of storytelling.[3] The most frequent musical form heard in African cultures was the song, ranging from lullabies to ritualized spirituals, and characterized by highly developed rhythms and a complex organization of sounds.[4]

Many songs and verses have been documented by and about African Americans. The former slave Olaudah Equiano wrote a description of life in Guinea in which he speaks proudly of the importance of music and dancing in the life of his people: "We are almost a nation of dancers, musicians, and poets. Thus every great event, such as a triumphant return from battle . . . is celebrated in public dances, which are accompanied with songs and music suited to the occasion."[5] Musical instruments, including stringed and percussion instruments, xylophone, harp, and flute, were well known in Africa. In the eighteenth-century watercolor *The Old Plantation,* the figures are shown performing the juba, a dance common to the Yoruba people (figure 1).[6] It also shows them playing instruments found in African cultures—the "molo," a type of banjo, for instance—and beating rhythm on a bowl drum.[7]

Former slaves remember the urge to express themselves in music, even when it was dangerous to do so.

FIGURE 1. Artist unknown, probably South Carolina. *The Old Plantation,* c. 1795. Watercolor on laid paper, 11 x 17 in. (27.9 x 43.2 cm). Abby Aldrich Rockefeller Folk Art Museum, The Colonial Williamsburg Foundation, Williamsburg, VA.

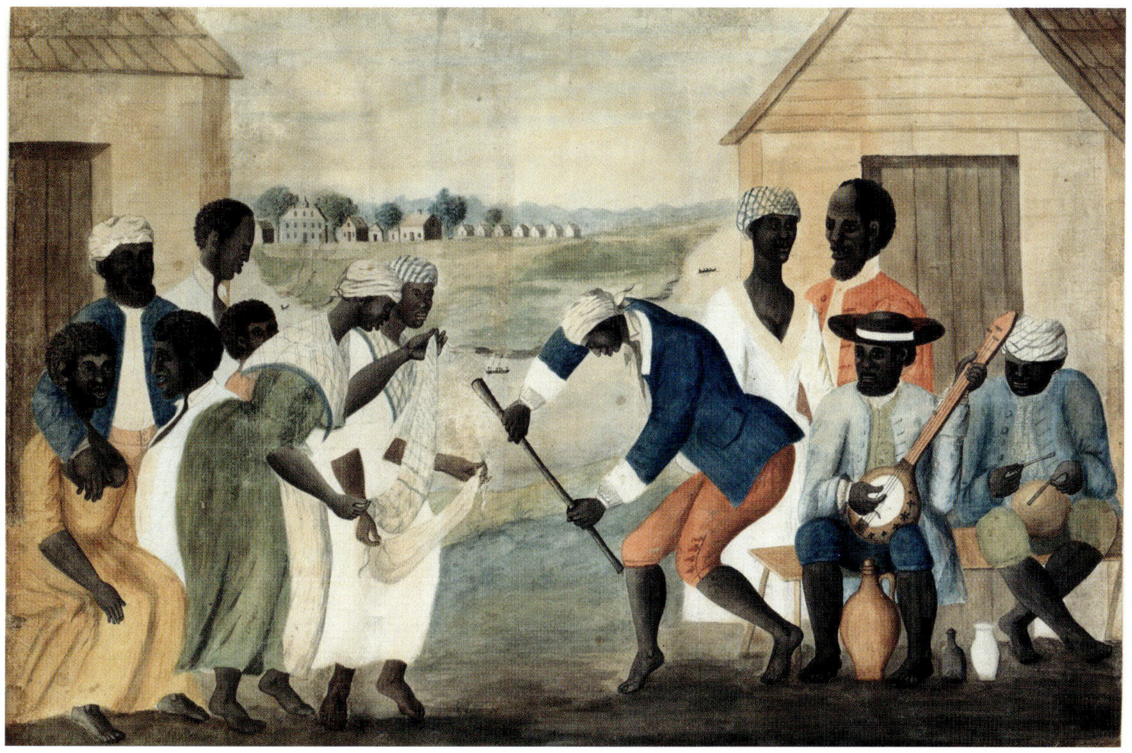

Hush, hush, boys,
Don't make a noise,
Massa's fast a-sleepin'.
Run to de barnyard,
Wake up de boys,
Let's have a banjo pickin'.[8]

FIGURE 2. *The Fugitive's Song,* 1845. Sheet music cover. Lithograph on wove paper, 14 x 9 3/8 in. (35.6 x 23.8 cm). Library of Congress, Prints and Photographs Division, LC-USZ62-7823.

Music and singing took on a far more important role in slave life than just the pleasure of sound or aesthetics of rhythm. Because conversations among the workers in the fields were prohibited, slaves used the lyrics in songs, both overtly and covertly, as a means of communication among themselves. They passed along messages in verse to control the pace of work or to subtly comment on a person or situation. In the fields, group participation in singing was common, often led by one individual who set the rhythm and cadence with a work song that started an entire group moving in unison.[9]

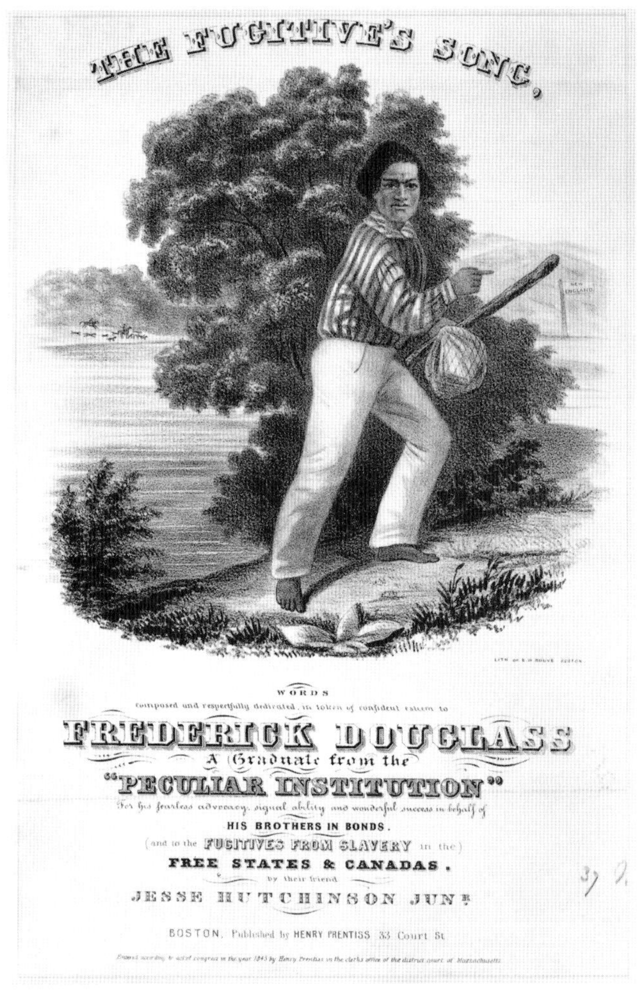

It is well documented that Harriet Tubman used songs such as "Bound for the Promised Land" and "Steal Away" to inform of an impending escape.[10] Harriet Tubman was called "the Moses of her people,"[11] perhaps in part because of the verses she sang to those who sought her help in their efforts to escape. The lyrics often referred to Moses as a metaphor for Tubman as she was leading her people out of bondage. She embedded instructions, directions, and caution in the words of her songs; their true meaning went undetected by anyone who overheard them. In one example she warns of impending danger:

Moses go down in Egypt,
Tell ole Pharaoh let me go;
Hadn't been for Adam's fall,
Shouldn't have to die at all.[12]

The reference to Adam's fall is a message to wait; danger is near.

Frederick Douglass, escaped slave, orator, and renowned antislavery activist, is portrayed on a sheet music cover for *The Fugitive's Song,* published in 1845 (figure 2). The text describes him as "Frederick Douglass, A Graduate from the 'Peculiar Institution.'"[13] He is shown as a young man at the edge of a river, fleeing barefoot from two mounted pursuers who are behind him across the river with their dogs. Douglass appears strong and heroic as he strides confidently toward a sign directing him north.

In a similar theme, but with a distinctly different perception of a fugitive, *In the Swamp* conveys a more sinister view (figure 3). The slave is huddled in the grass, frightened and terrified, as his mounted pursuers and their dogs close in and a successful escape seems in jeopardy.[14]

While music played an important role in inspiring Holston, it shares equal gravity with the power of color. In fact, it is perhaps the combination of the two that is most significant to Holston's style, in which color can be perceived as sound. Holston translates the dialogue between the tonal values of pigment and the tonal quality of musical notes.

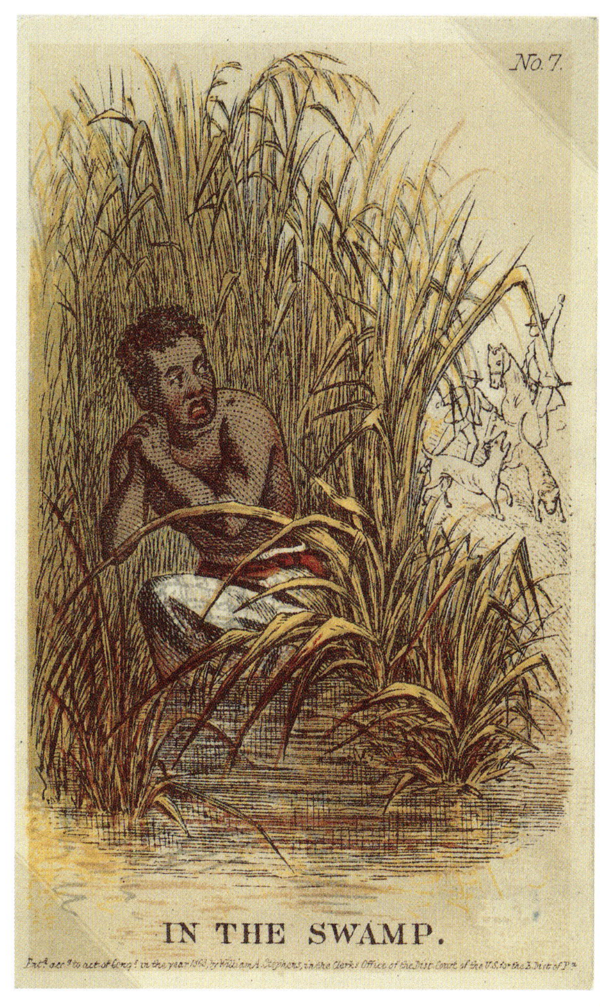

FIGURE 3. H. L. (Henry Louis) Stephens (American, 1824–1882). *In the Swamp,* c. 1863. Color lithograph. Library of Congress, Prints and Photographs Division, LC-USZC4-2522.

Scientists have long studied the neurologically based phenomenon called *synesthesia,* in which stimulation of one sensory or cognitive pathway leads to automatic or involuntary experience in a second sensory pathway.[15] With color synesthesia, individuals experience colors in response to hearing tones or other musical stimuli. Studies have suggested that people experience higher pitched notes as more brightly colored. Holston's paintings capture the essence of color synesthesia, as the viewer experiences the sensation of colors moving, or streaming in and out of the field of vision.[16]

Wassily Kandinsky, the twentieth-century Russian pioneer of abstraction, took the concept of color and sound even further when he declared his firm belief in the "deep relationship between the arts and especially between music and painting."[17] Explaining in detail, he relayed how he was convinced that colors were heard and that the perceived sound directly affected the emotional iconography of a painting. "Color is a power which directly influences the soul. Color is the keyboard, the eyes are the hammers, the soul is the piano with many strings. The artist is the hand which plays, touching one key or another, to cause vibrations in the soul."[18]

Kandinsky revealed his systematic order of primary and secondary colors associated with the sounds of certain instruments in *Fragment 2 for Composition VII,* 1913 (figure 4). He explained that yellow is allied with the sound of a trumpet, orange with that of a viola, red with the sound of a drum, and blue with that of a cello. He was careful to organize the colors in repetitive patterns, to mimic an echo or reverberation as it may be heard from each musical instrument. Kandinsky is well respected for his romantic view that colors have a psychic as well as a visual effect. "[Colors] produce a corresponding spiritual vibration, and it is only as a step towards this spiritual vibration that the elementary physical impression is of importance."[19]

FIGURE 4. Wassily Kandinsky (Russian, 1866–1944). *Fragment 2 for Composition VII,* 1913. Oil on canvas, 34½ x 39¼ in. (87.6 x 99.7 cm). Albright-Knox Art Gallery, Buffalo, New York. Room of Contemporary Art Fund, 1947.

American artist Stanton Macdonald-Wright, sympathetic to Kandinsky's theory, cofounded the art movement Synchromism. His philosophy was based on the idea that color and sound produce similar phenomena and that painting in "color scales," using rhythmic color and repetitive form, results in a central vortex of complex color harmonies in the same way that musical scales evoke audio sensations.[20]

A prime example of this style is his painting *Conception Synchromy,* 1914 (figure 5). He combined multicolored shapes overlapping in an abstract nonobjective composition. His effort to perceive form as liberated from objective subject matter is, in his view, a means to "unlock the secrets of nature and to bring painting to a supreme degree of harmonic intensity."[21]

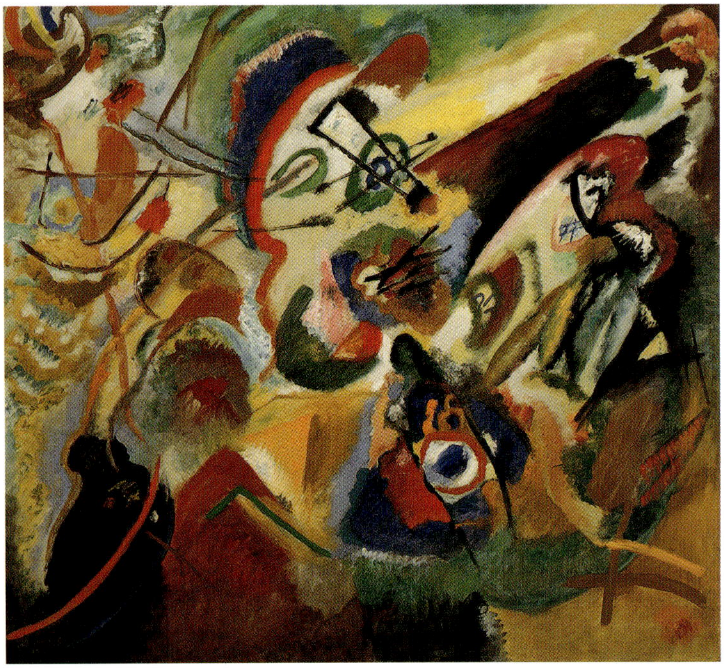

In keeping with the legacy of these earlier art movements, Holston takes his principles of color theory and musical harmony even further. He combines the fundamentals of synesthesia and Synchromism and adds his own vision of color and form. They become the starting point for a whole series of related sensations that bring the viewer into personal contact with an objective context of the subject matter. In Holston's hands, the colors acquire an inner meaning and, eventually, a spiritual harmony, moving the viewer closer to the emotional content appropriate to the sensitive subjects portrayed.

The power of color on Holston's palette is enhanced by his use of bold lines. The painting *Responsibility of Freedom* (figure 6), with its figures juxtaposed in saturated hues both warm and cool, demonstrates his grasp of the strength of color intensity and the power of overlapping forms. The rhythmic lines resonate and seem to vibrate in space.

The body of work in this exhibition unites Holston's distinctive technique, style, and iconography to convey a message of strength, power, perseverance, and courage. The images interpret one of the most egregious periods in American history. Holston puts a human face on the historical narrative and brings the personal struggles to life.

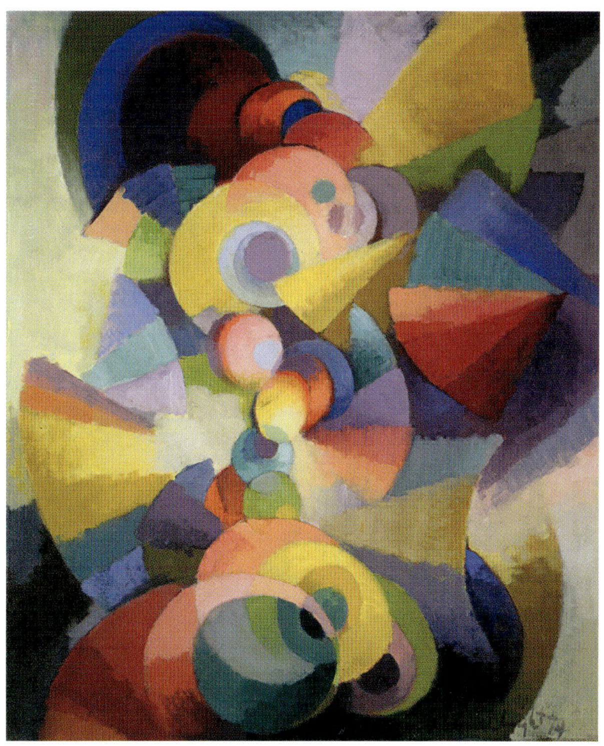

FIGURE 5. Stanton Macdonald-Wright (American, 1890–1973). *Conception Synchromy,* 1914. Oil on canvas, 36 x 30 1/8 in. (91.3 x 76.5 cm). Hirshhorn Museum and Sculpture Garden, Smithsonian Institution, Gift of Joseph H. Hirshhorn, 1966. Photographer: Lee Stalsworth.

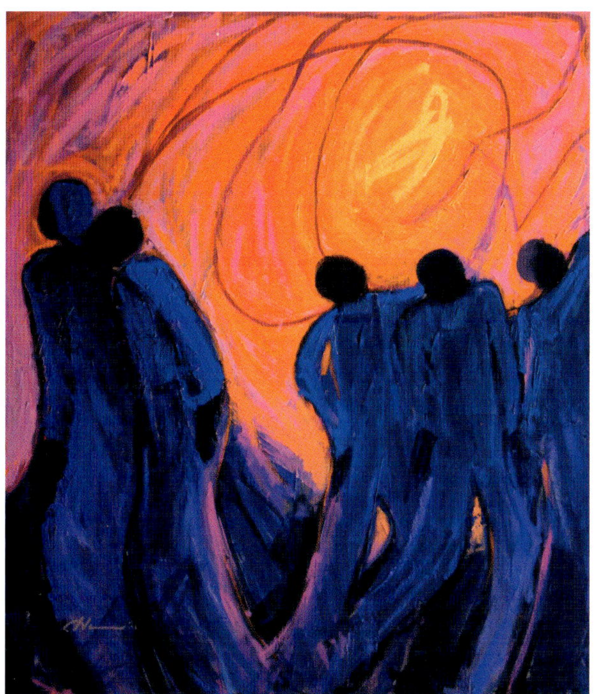

FIGURE 6. *Responsibility of Freedom*

Notes

1. Frederick Douglass, *Narrative of the Life of Frederick Douglass, an American Slave,* with introduction by Kwame Anthony Appiah (New York: Modern Library, 2000), 49. Originally published in 1845. Frederick Douglass (1818–1895) escaped from slavery, fleeing in 1838 from Maryland to Massachusetts. He achieved considerable renown for his autobiography.
2. Karin V. Maur, *The Sound of Painting: Music in Modern Art,* trans. John W. Gabriel (Munich: Prestel, 1999).
3. James Oliver Horton and Lois E. Horton, *Slavery and the Making of America* (New York: Oxford University Press, 2005), 41.
4. John Hope Franklin and Alfred A. Moss Jr., *From Slavery to Freedom: A History of Negro Americans,* 6th ed. (New York: Knopf, 1987), 22.
5. Ibid., 9. Olaudah Equiano (c. 1745–1797), also known as Gustavus Vassa, was one of the most prominent people of African heritage involved in the British debate for the abolition of the slave trade. After becoming a free black living in London, he wrote an autobiography that depicted the horrors of slavery and helped influence British lawmakers to abolish the slave trade in 1807. In addition to being a slave as a young man, he was also a seaman, a merchant, and an explorer in the Caribbean, the American colonies, Britain, and the North Pole.
6. Horton and Horton, *Slavery and the Making of America,* 41. The phrase *patting juba* is often seen in accounts of plantation life and refers to patting the rhythm of this dance on one's knee in the absence of a musical instrument.
7. Leo G. Mazow, *Picturing the Banjo* (University Park: Pennsylvania State University Press, 2005); John Henry Drewel and John Pemberton III, *Yoruba: Nine Centuries of African Art and Thought* (New York: Abrams, 1989).
8. Norman R. Yetman, ed., *Voices from Slavery: 100 Authentic Slave Narratives* (Mineola, NY: Dover, 2000), 114.
9. Horton and Horton, *Slavery and the Making of America,* 125. Some of the lyrics communicated messages of unrest and escape planning. Examples are "people get ready, there's a train a-comin'," "beyond dis vale of sorrow," and "de fields of endless days."
10. Ibid., 138. Reprinted from Earl Conrad, *General Harriet Tubman* (Washington, DC: Associated Publishers, 1943). Harriet Tubman (c. 1820–1913) was born into slavery in Dorchester County, Maryland, and escaped to Philadelphia in 1849, only to make repeated return missions to help fugitive slaves escape using the network of antislavery activists and safe houses known as the Underground Railroad. She later helped John Brown recruit men for his raid on Harpers Ferry, and in the postwar era she struggled for women's suffrage.
11. Catherine Clinton, *Harriet Tubman: The Road to Freedom* (New York: Little, Brown & Co., 2004), 79.
12. Beverly Lowry, *Harriet Tubman: Imagining a Life* (New York: Doubleday, 2007), 180.
13. The full text states: "The Fugitive's Song, composed and respectfully dedicated, in token of confident esteem, to Frederick Douglass. A graduate from the 'peculiar institution.' For his fearless advocacy, signal ability and wonderful success in behalf of his brothers in bonds. (and to the fugitives from slavery in the) free states & Canadas, by their friend Jesse Hutchinson Junr." As the illustration suggests, Douglass was himself a fugitive. See also note 1 above. John C. Calhoun used the term *peculiar institution* publicly in 1837, in a speech in support of slavery.
14. Twenty years after Douglass's image was published, in the midst of the Civil War, small cards such as this were sold to support the antislavery movement and raise funds for the Union cause.
15. *Synesthesia* is from the ancient Greek *syn,* meaning "with," and *aesthesis,* meaning "sensation." Recent studies of synesthesia include J. Ward, E. Tsakanikos, and A. Bray, "Synaesthesia for reading and playing musical notes," *Neurocase* 12 (1): 27–34, and J. Simner and E. Holenstein, "Ordinal linguistic personification as a variant of synesthesia," *Journal of Cognitive Neuroscience* 19 (4): 694–703.
16. Faber Birren, *Color and Human Response: Aspects of Light and Color Bearing on the Reactions of Living Things and the Welfare of Human Beings* (New York: Wiley, 2005), v. Birren is considered one of the leading authorities on the psychological, visual, and physiological function of color and its effects on the human psyche.
17. Wassily Kandinsky, *Concerning the Spiritual in Art* (Mineola, NY: Dover, 1977), 23. Originally published as *The Art of Spiritual Harmony* (1914). Wassily Kandinsky (1866–1944), credited with the first abstract painting, was founder with Franz Marc of the group Der Blaue Reiter ("The Blue Rider") in 1911.
18. Ibid., 25.
19. Ibid., 36.
20. Maur, *Sound of Painting,* 22. Stanton Macdonald-Wright (1890–1973) developed the style called Synchromism with Morgan Russell (1886–1953) while studying in Paris in 1907. The first Synchromist painting, by Russell, was titled *Synchromy in Green* and was exhibited in Paris at the Salon des Indépendants in 1913. After a brief stay in London, Macdonald-Wright moved to the United States, where he would exhibit his work for the rest of his life. Other American painters experimenting with Synchromism included Thomas Hart Benton (1889–1975), Andrew Dasburg (1887–1979), and Patrick Henry Bruce (1881–1936).
21. Ibid., 26.

THE FIRST MOVEMENT

The Unknown World

> The entire New World enterprise depended on the enormous and expandable flow of slave labor from Africa.
>
> DAVID BRION DAVIS[1]

The first movement in the journey through the exhibition begins with Holston's artistic interpretation of the world from which the enslaved Africans were taken. In most African regions, the security and prosperity of the community rested with the power of the tribal king. The system by which he governed was well organized under a hierarchical structure, maintaining regional order and stability.[2] Removed abruptly from their communities and homes, kidnapped Africans found themselves facing an uncertain future of lifelong servitude in a foreign and hostile environment.

In *Protection* (figure 7), Holston captures the regal and authoritative countenance of a ruler, someone who represented a father figure and who was, no doubt, on the minds of the captives. He is portrayed as large, stately, and imperial. Rendered in a white tunic against a bold background, he blends into his surroundings with a fusion of red-orange framing his head, bordered by chevron patterns that decorate the sides of his throne and echo the peaks at the top of his crown. He symbolizes the vision most of the displaced would carry with them, a memory of the grandeur and splendor of the homeland and all it evoked. The large, capable hands emerge majestically, enveloping his subjects in safety and security.

In its direct reference to exhilaration and triumph, Holston's color choice is deliberate rather than fortuitous. The colors gold, red, and orange have been universally associated with bountiful opulence as well as with power and authority. A popular notion among artists and color theorists was: "Everyone knows that yellow [gold], orange, and red suggest ideas of joy and plenty."[3] In this case, it is not only the color that adds strength to the image, but also the compositional harmony and balance, with forceful directional lines symbolizing the order and structure that represent the imperial sovereignty of a leader.

The composition is structured to send a powerful message of benevolent compassion and inflexible strength. Consider the imposing force of the triangle or pyramidal form created by the dark tones of the hands, arms, and face, topped literally by a crown reminding us of the regal monarch we behold. The deep rich hue juxtaposed with the bright background tone emphasizes the validity of his rule.

The forced deportation of Africans from their homeland brought them to North America as early as the 1560s, where they appeared on inventory lists in Spanish Florida.[4] The conditions aboard slave ships were "probably too horrible to fully convey in human words."[5]

An eighteenth-century etching (figure 8) shows a diagram of the typical arrangement of "cargo" on slave ships, where the prisoners were densely packed in the decks between the ship's bottom and the main level. Conditions aboard such ships were wretched and the atmosphere inhumane. The slave traders depended on this kind of brutal treatment and exploitation to subdue their captives before reaching "market" in the New World. Thus began a system of "collective degradation" that facilitated racism and sustained slavery for so many decades.[6]

FIGURE 7. *Protection*

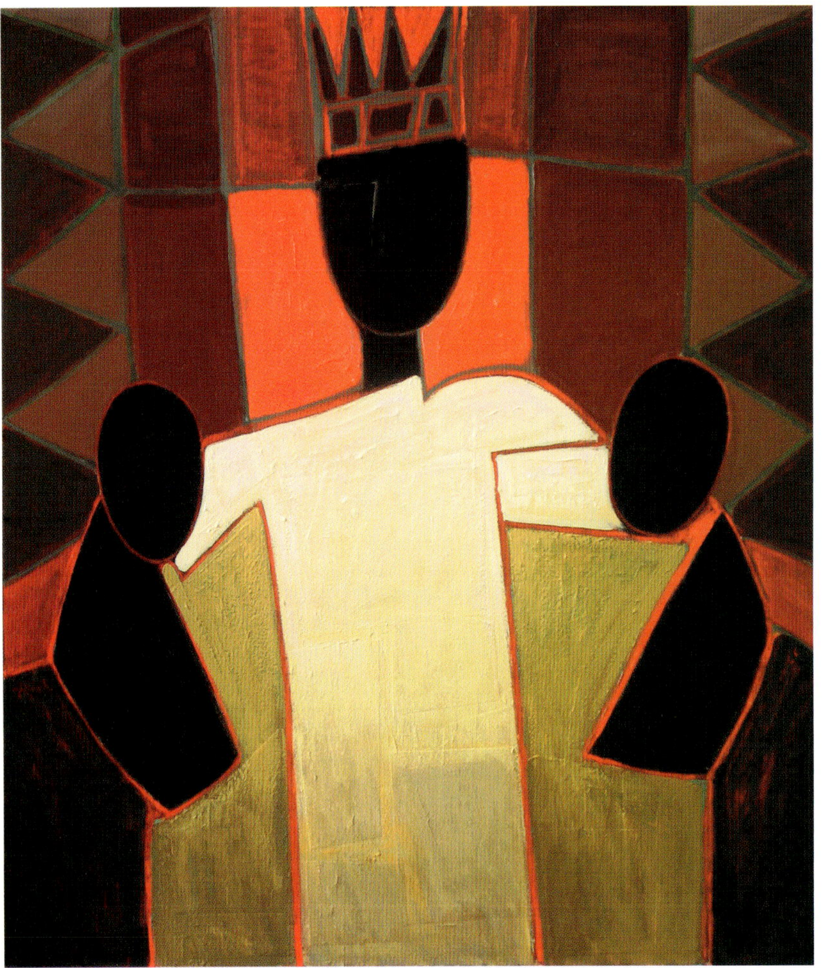

In *Arrival in the Unknown* (figure 9), Holston captures the essence of how the people who made the arduous passage were forced to remain closely locked together in tight quarters with no room to stand or move about. Below deck they would be subjected to unspeakable treatment, with little food, water, or fresh air to breathe as they endured the long voyage to North America. The painting expresses these conditions with a series of overlapping lines and a distinct absence of space between figures. There is no depth perception beyond the ship, and the figures are forced together and thrust en masse to the foreground: a pictorial organization that echoes the suffering of the "passengers" of a typical slave ship. The closeness is not intimate or familial; rather, it expresses the degradation of individuality and the debasement of dignity, inviolable rights that will be forever denied to these souls.

In *Subjugation* (figure 10), the composition maintains the close physical juxtaposition of the captives. Here they find themselves in a situation that is only a little improved over the horrors of the voyage. The connection between them is clearly not compatible or comfortable. Despite the physical closeness, they do not relate or communicate; it is almost as if they know that attempted discourse would acknowledge a loss of self, a relinquishing of their individual freedom once and for all. The gravity of participating in the loss of one's own freedom was argued by Samuel Sewall in his first antislavery treatise: "Forasmuch as Liberty is in real value next unto Life: None ought to part with it themselves, or deprive others of it."[7] Holston's figures remain stationary and rigid, demoralized by the loss of humanity, dignity, heritage, and family. The three figures are literally linked in the rhythmic, repetitive loop of the

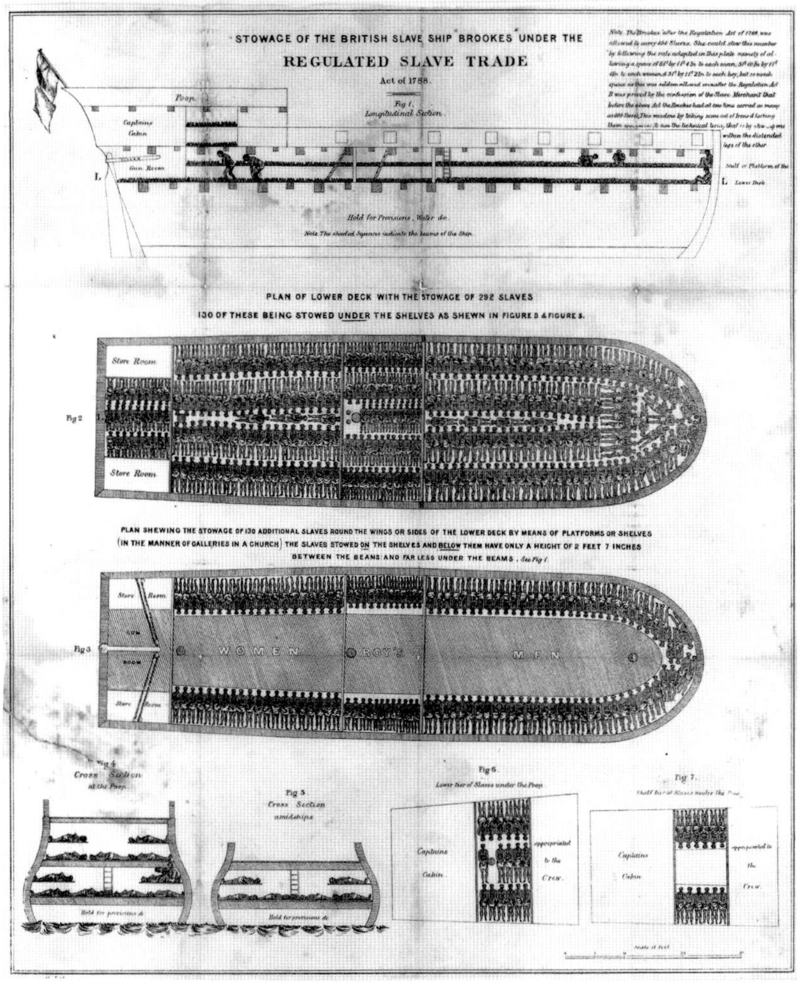

FIGURE 8. *Stowage of the British slave ship Brookes under the regulated slave trade act of 1788.* Etching. Library of Congress, Prints and Photographs Division, LC-USZ62-44000.

chains that bind them together, forever linking their destiny. They are composed as a single, massive form filling the picture plane, suggesting a strength and solidarity that belies their captivity. This organization rejects the idea of a separate identity; rather, it suggests a collective portrait of the forced debasement and degrading humiliation imposed on an entire race. The brutal treatment and exploitation would only become worse as the situation progressed toward a lifelong ordeal of bondage.

A line parallel to the waistlines of the men stretches horizontally across the middle of the canvas, marking the division of space behind the figures. Dark blue frames their upper torsos and bright orange encases their lower bodies. These powerful background colors are a brilliant choice of contrast. The combination of blue and orange brings a tempo to the pattern change and a compatibility that strengthens each color, adding credence to the theory that harmony requires complements, referring to complementary colors in the color circle, where, for example, orange demands blue to acquire its full potential and true strength.[8]

FIGURE 9.
Arrival in the Unknown

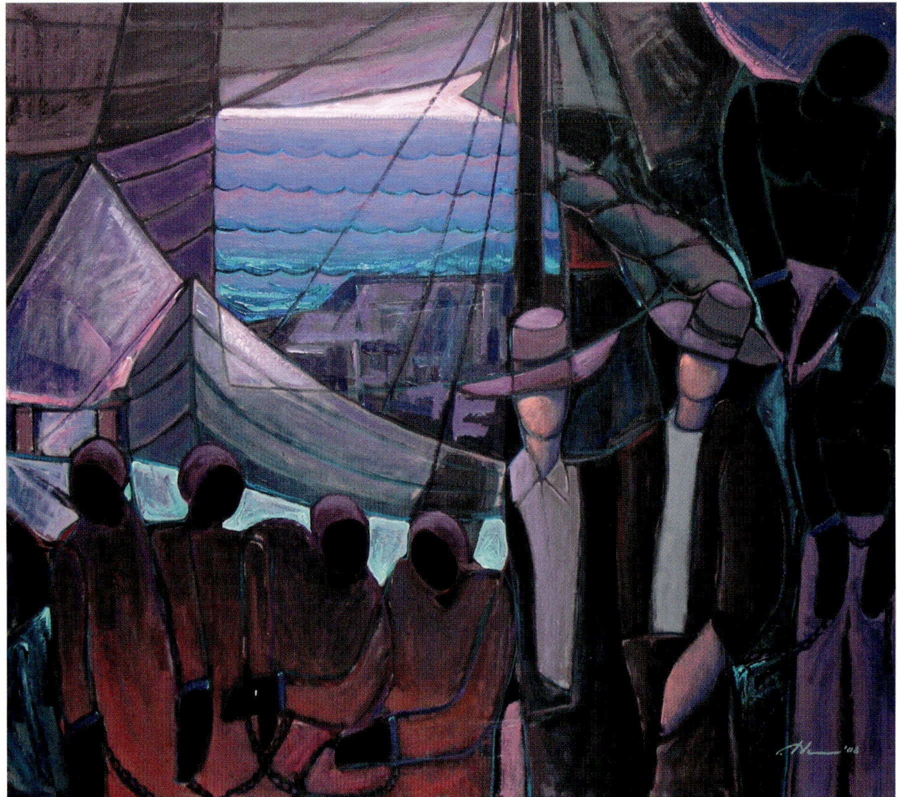

The forms overlap, leaving no space between them, and yet the psychological distance keeps them segregated from each other and from their surroundings. It is likely that they would have been from different tribes or different parts of Africa. "African" as a nationality did not exist on the continent of Africa. People were identified by their tribal heritage, but that distinction was not recognized in America, where *African* simply meant "of African descent."[9] They would not have shared the same system of communication or behavior patterns. The common language that ultimately developed among the slave population was, for the most part, a "medley of African dialects and English."[10]

By contrast, *Middle Passage* (figure 11) depicts the figures on their knees and shackled separately. There is no physical connection between these men, no overlapping as each is pulled in a different direction. They each seem to dwell within a personal, introspective misery; there is no mass or solidarity here. The forms behind them swirl in a deep gray to pale yellow kaleidoscope of color, adding to a feeling of dizziness and confusion. The focal point is the central figure that divides the composition in half diagonally. He projects forward into the viewer's space, drawing attention to the strong, muscular upper body that is, nevertheless, so helplessly confined as to be unable to move about freely. There is a dichotomy between the simplicity of the deliberate lines around the flat forms and the complexity of the iconographical implication in this composition. It is perhaps a metaphor for the cultural system that would, in due course, isolate the South and ultimately divide the nation.[11]

FIGURE 10.
Subjugation

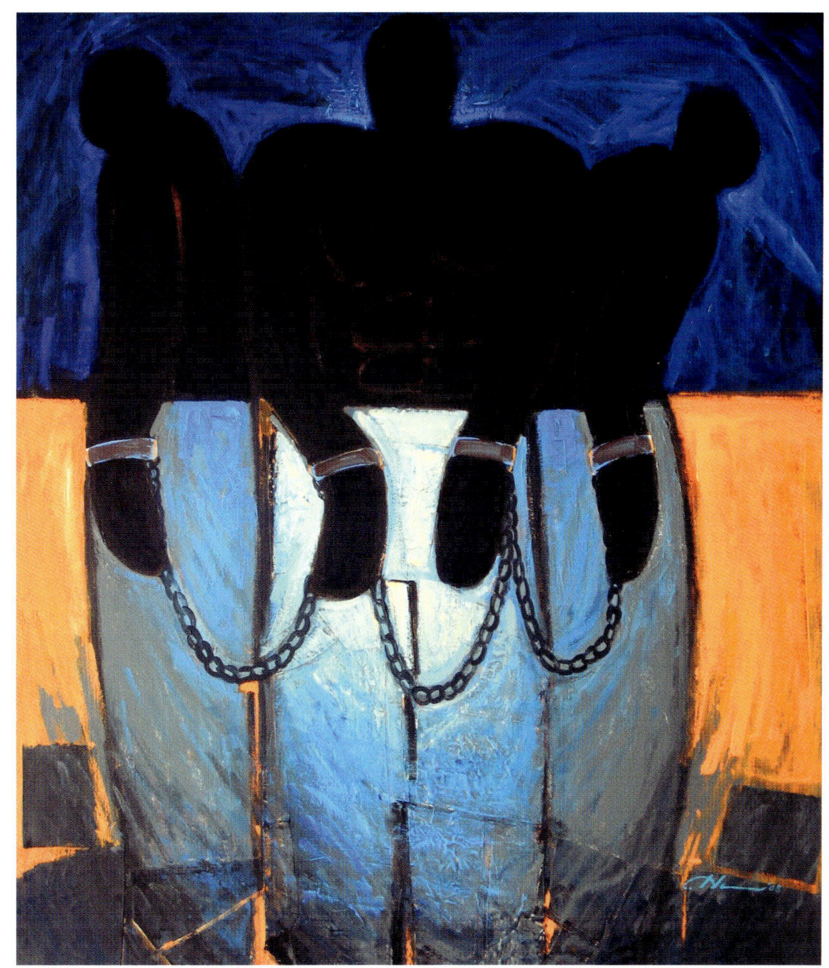

Historians have referred to the first group of slaves to arrive in America as the "Charter Generation."[12] By creating alliances with other slaves whose language and customs were as foreign to them as those of their captors, most provided a mechanism for survival that endured through many generations of American-born slaves. Holston's paintings depict the strength and innate drive that can survive under any circumstances. Isaac Williams, a former slave from Virginia, tells a long story of strife and depravity, but concludes with a dream in which he hears a voice telling him, "As long as there's breath there's hope."[13]

As Holston guides us through the early years of American slavery, his paintings convey the hardships and disappointments that many encountered along the way. Through subdued and unifying forms interacting with deliberate linear organization, he brings an imaginative and perceptive message to the core of the story of enslavement. Each composition celebrates survival as it deliberately illustrates a psychic example of the inner meaning derived from the strength it would require. For most black slaves, "seeking black survival was equal to attaining white power."[14] They knew intuitively that they had the advantage over their captors because while "white folks had the power, black folks survived."[15]

FIGURE 11.
Middle Passage

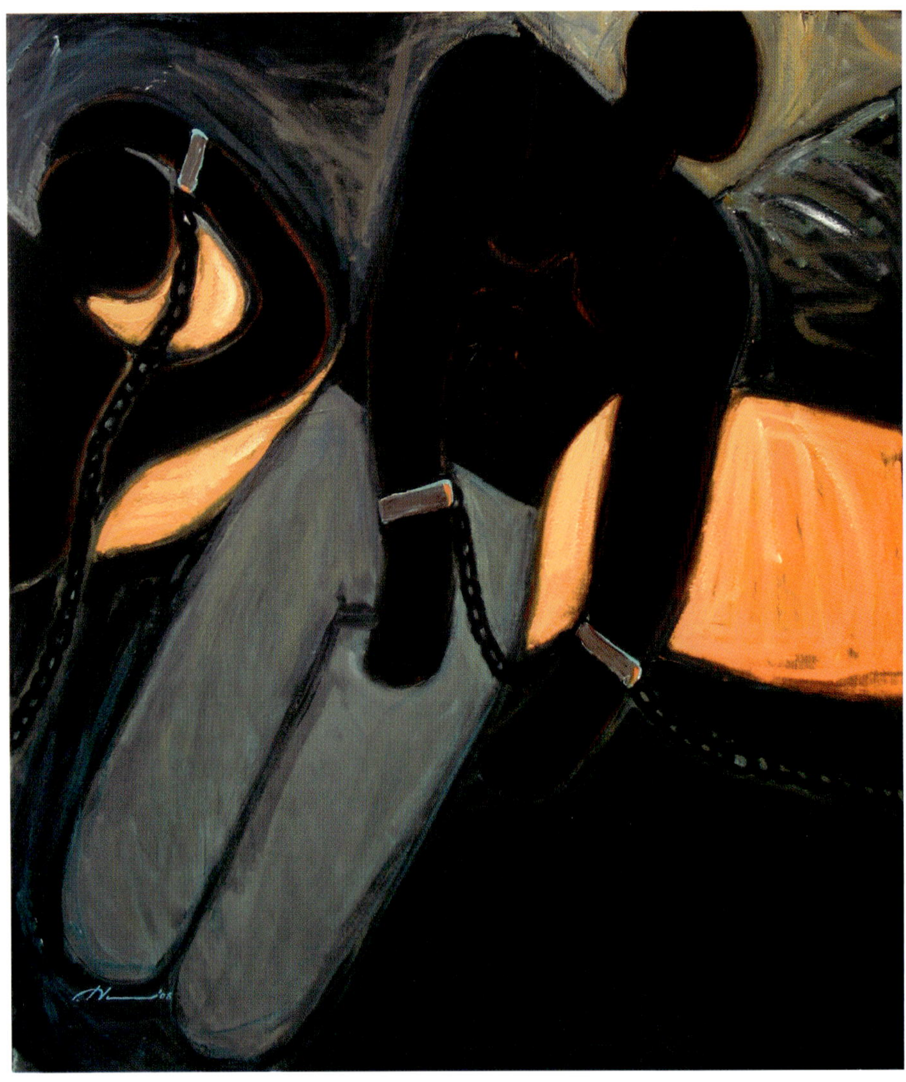

Notes

1. David Brion Davis, *Inhuman Bondage: The Rise and Fall of Slavery in the New World* (New York: Oxford University Press, 2006), 80.
2. Paul Edwards, ed., *The Interesting Narrative of the Life of Olaudah Equiano, or Gustavus Vassa, the African* (New York: Norton Critical Editions, 2000). Originally published by Olaudah Equiano in 1789. See also note 5, p. 20.
3. Wassily Kandinsky, *Concerning the Spiritual in Art* (Mineola, NY: Dover, 1977), 24.
4. Davis, *Inhuman Bondage,* 125. The area of modern-day Florida was known as Spanish Florida when the Spanish established a colony there in 1565. It came under British rule in 1763 and remained so until after the American Revolution.
5. Ibid., 92.
6. Ibid., 135.
7. David Hackett Fischer, *Liberty and Freedom: A Visual History of America's Founding Ideas* (New York: Oxford University Press, 2004), 275. In *The Selling of Joseph* (1700), Samuel Sewall (1652–1730) came out strongly against slavery, making him one of the earliest colonial abolitionists.
8. Faber Birren, *Color and Human Response: Aspects of Light and Color Bearing on the Reactions of Living Things and the Welfare of Human Beings* (New York: Wiley, 2005), 75. Birren quotes the foremost nineteenth-century color theorists, Johann Wolfgang von Goethe and Michel-Eugène Chevreul, who wrote about the phenomenon of simultaneous contrast, or afterimage. "In the case where the eye sees at the same time two contiguous colors, they will appear as dissimilar as possible, both in their optical composition and in the height of their tone."
9. David Blight, ed., *Passages to Freedom: The Underground Railroad in History and Memory* (New York: Smithsonian Books/HarperCollins, in association with the National Underground Railroad Freedom Center, 2004), 30.
10. Ibid., 20.
11. Fischer, *Liberty and Freedom,* 288. In *Freedom-of-Thought Struggles in the Old South* (1940), Clement Eaton (1898–1980), historian of the American South, wrote about the repressive silence that rendered the Southern plantation states increasingly isolated behind what he called "the cotton curtain."
12. Blight, *Passages to Freedom,* 14. Subsequent generations were referred to as the "Plantation Generation" and later the "Revolution Generation."
13. Benjamin Drew, *The Narratives of Fugitive Slaves* (Toronto: Prospero, 2000), 63. Originally published in 1856 by John P. Jewett & Co. Isaac Williams made his escape from Virginia in 1854. Drew interviewed former slaves in many Canadian cities in 1855. In the introduction to his published narratives, he says he found that for most "the oppression of the laboring portion of the community amounts to an entire deprivation of their civil and personal rights . . . [but] found [this] inadequate to hold in check the natural desire of liberty" (1).
14. Blight, *Passages to Freedom,* 65.
15. Ibid., 33.

THE SECOND MOVEMENT

Living in Bondage—Life on the Plantation

> I was brought up in ignorance.
> I felt put down—oppressed in spirit.
>
> MRS. ELLIS[1]

The second movement in the exhibition, *Living in Bondage,* addresses the struggles of adapting to life on the plantation. It represents the overture in this continuing journey, an independent movement in the extended symphonic composition. The drama of the images sets the tempo for the struggle that will unfold. The tempo in painting shares a crucial importance with its counterpart in musical sound; it determines the pace or time and can affect the mood and difficulty of a given piece.

Holston balances the formal proportions conveying fortitude, perseverance, and strength with the bold, blunt reality of the horrific conditions of forced bondage and servitude. The suffering was unimaginable and can be truly understood only by those who endured it. Many have lent their voices to express the fear, sorrow, and contempt they felt as slaves as well as the hope, promise, and faith that kept them alive. Christopher Nichols remembers, "All the time I was in slavery, I lived in dead dread and fear. If I slept it was in dread—and in the morning it was dread—dread, night and day."[2] John Atkinson spoke of the constant longing for freedom: "A man who has been in slavery knows, and no one else can know, the yearnings to be free, and the fear of making the attempt. It is like trying to get religion, and not seeing the way to escape condemnation."[3] After several unsuccessful attempts, Henry Bibb achieved freedom in 1837 and became an antislavery activist. He wrote his story in 1849, stating, "I was a slave, a prisoner for life; I could possess nothing, nor acquire anything but what must belong to my keeper. No one can imagine my feelings in my reflecting moments, but he who has himself been a slave."[4]

In Holston's images of this period, there is always a light present, a light that lends hope and energy, allowing slaves to believe in their ultimate success and freedom. In *Dawn of Despair* (figure 12), the figures create a single strong, unyielding mass across the canvas. While they sit in deep shadow with their heads down in subjugation and their backs bowed in fatigue, the overlarge sun (light) above is ever present. It fills the upper canvas and seems to press down on the backs of the men, yet they do not look up. Is it that they don't see it, or that they can't acknowledge it? While the light is reflected on their backs, they refuse, or are unable, to bask in its warmth. This is, perhaps, an analogy for the life of a slave who is surrounded by the pleasures of nature but restricted from appreciation of or participation in its bounty.

By contrast, the figures in *Betimes* (figure 13) separate themselves and occupy individual spaces. Each figure is precisely delineated, and they echo one another's gestures as they twist and turn in unison. The unified swaying movement of the group presents a rhythm of sorts and facilitates the figures as they raise themselves up, both literally and figuratively. The dark cloud that extends across the upper canvas slowly gives way to the sun (light) hovering just above their heads and reflecting its warmth with rays of hope as their backs unfurl to suggest the promise of a brighter day. The two to the left reach toward each other, a clear sign of moving toward a coalition of spirit.

There were those who refused to abandon their "spirit or be broken by the violence" and cruelty of their existence.[5] For those who were required to work in the fields from sunup to sundown, learning to pace oneself with a steady cadence of motion and tempo was paramount for survival. Austin Steward, a freed slave writing in 1857, recorded the details of starting a typical workday in bondage: "They [slaves] were usually found in the fields 'betimes in the morning,' where they worked until nine o'clock. They were then allowed thirty minutes to eat their morning meal, which consisted of a little bread. At a given signal, all hands were

FIGURE 12.
Dawn of Despair

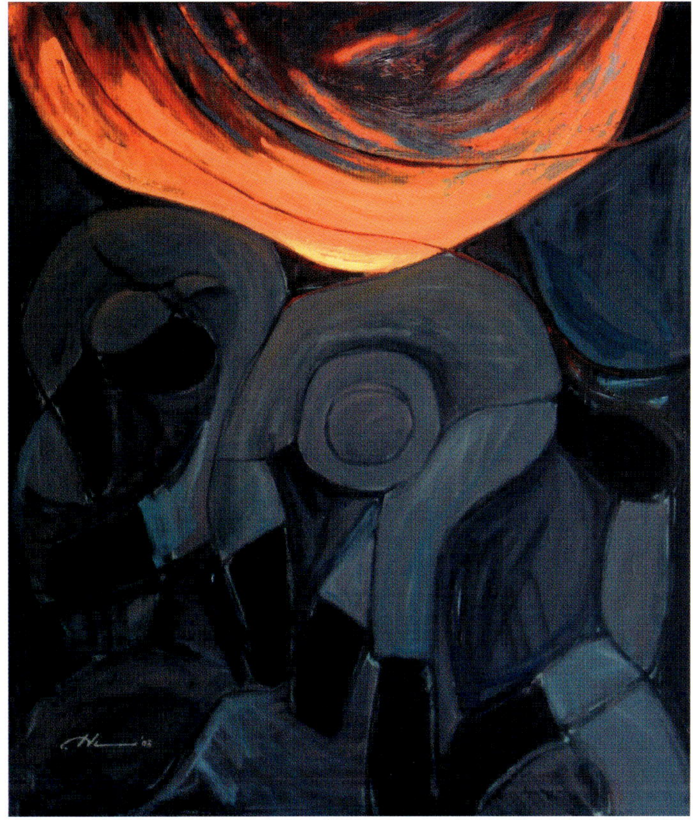

compelled to return to their work. They toiled until noon, when they were permitted to take their breakfast, which corresponds to our dinner."[6] *Betimes* is an old Virginia term meaning to be on time or face the wrath of the overseer—failure to meet the work timeline could result in severe punishment.[7]

Holston shows us a poetic rhythm in *Private Plot* (figure 14), rendering the background with flowing, undulating lines interrupted only by the diagonal line piercing the foreground and connecting the man to the earth and to the task upon which he is so focused. As he steadily works, the soil seems to ascend upward to the left, engulfing the houses and wedging them up against the hills behind. His chore is tedious, the mood is dispiriting, as he steals a private moment to toil in his own plot of land. But Holston penetrates the blue and gray tones with the ever-present light above. It divides the hills and descends to actually touch the worker while he labors, prompting an expectation of better days to come. Can the light of hope "move mountains" to bring justice to the oppressed?

Women were expected to labor as hard as men and were equally as vulnerable to abuses. Enslaved women had no legal rights and no defense against personal injury or assault. They had no protection from the malevolent overtures of their owners.

FIGURE 13. *Betimes*

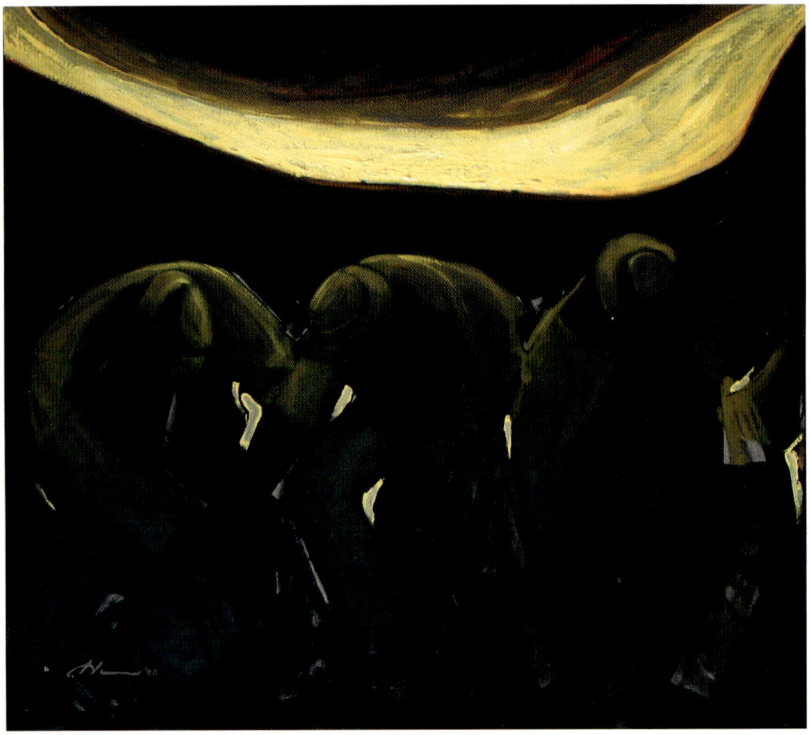

Holston captures the foreboding and threatening atmosphere that was part of a slave woman's everyday existence in *Rape* (figure 15). As the male figure leans in toward the woman, she is shown in profile, turning slightly away from her assaulter. She holds her arms close to her breast, shielding herself from the dangers she knows she cannot escape. Henry Bibb recalls that "a poor slave's wife . . . can not be true to her husband contrary to the will of her master. She can neither be pure nor virtuous, contrary to the will of her master. She dare not refuse to be reduced to a state of adultery at the will of her master."[8] The menacing figure of the man, one who is dedicated to brutal savagery and cruelty to retain power and control, symbolizes not just an isolated predatory moment, but the sinister, terrifying state of slavery itself. The woman represents all those bound by suppression and subjugation, who are living not as individuals, but as the property of another. The light is present in this painting, but here it is subdued, and as the woman averts her eyes from its soft glow, it is clear she will not find solace or promise from it very soon.

Women, despite these conditions, created a sense of stability in home and hearth, a remarkable achievement in an atmosphere where oppression and cruelty were the norm. They found ways to create identity within communities for nuclear and extended families, and to stimulate and nurture lives under the harshest of conditions. Regardless of how tyrannical or demoralizing plantation life was, the struggle for survival was paramount, and women found unique cultural ways to lighten the burden for themselves and their families. Holston captures the reality of home life for the slave by rendering the simplicity and constancy of the woman's role in *Place of Respite* (figure 16).

We see the woman in a rare quiet, private moment. Holston uses compelling lines to guide the viewer around the scene. The vertical rectangle of the cabin, with the four smaller square windows, is the barrier that separates the viewer from the landscape beyond the yard. The small patch of light in the upper-right corner is just enough to cast a shimmer of bright hope on the woman. The arcing lines coming from the open door follow the bodies of the chickens horizontally across the lower foreground and curve upward to the left, where the woman assumes our attention. She is a strong presence as her body curves around the left perimeter of the canvas and she gently swings her arm to distribute feed to the chickens below. She turns her head to look at the proud, strutting birds, suggesting a connection to and empathy with the earth and the chickens—which may be among her meager personal possessions. Many enslaved people on plantations were responsible for providing their own food. Near their living quarters they had small plots

FIGURE 14. *Private Plot*

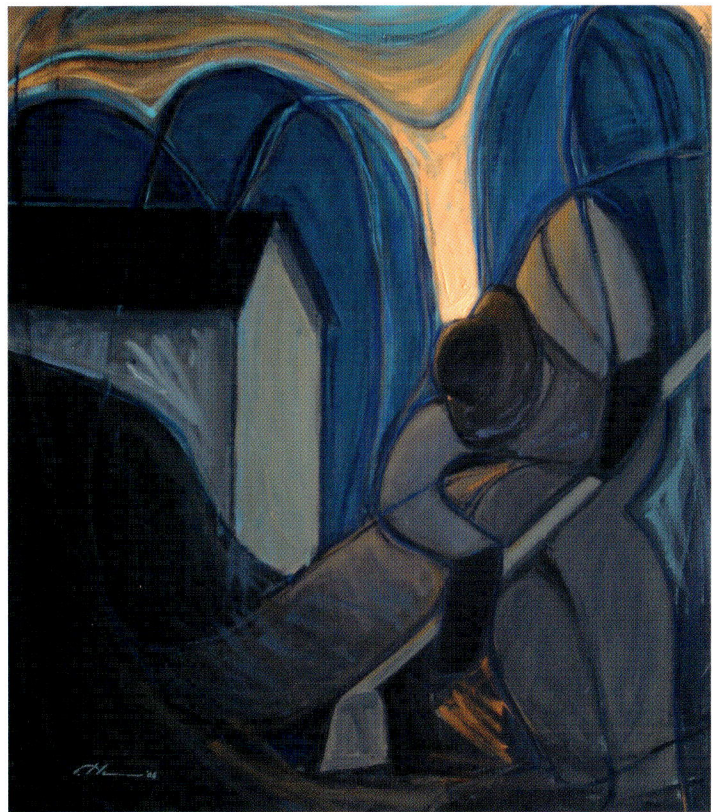

of land on which they grew modest crops, and some were fortunate enough to have cows or chickens to supplement their diet.

Hope was possibly at its dimmest when families were separated. The fear of separation from family was never far from the consciousness of those enslaved. Former slave George Johnson recalled, "Whipping and slashing are bad enough, but selling children from their mothers and husbands from their wives is worse."[9] It was well known that "a slave may be bought and sold in the market . . . He is liable to be sold off to a distant land from his family."[10] The innate right and responsibility to protect one's family was denied the enslaved. The practice was not uncommon, but those who suffered the consequences abhorred it no less. A former slave, Reverend Alexander Hemsley witnessed the family separation on many occasions and testified: "The unwillingness to separate of husbands and wives, parents and children was so great, that to part them seemed . . . a sin higher than the heavens."[11]

The sanctity of family is portrayed most powerfully in *Madonna and Child* (figure 17). Here Holston portrays not only a maternal bond between mother and child, but also the power of devotion and faith. The figure of the mother is large, filling the canvas with her presence and creating a barrier that shields the child from what she knows will be a hard and trying future. She reaches her hand tenderly and affectionately toward the child, who is tucked securely in the crook of her arm. Slave mothers, in spite of hardship and suffering, lavished tenderhearted love on their children. Mothers were known to work tirelessly to bolster the self-esteem of the children, a monumental task under the circumstances of bondage. They taught their children important lessons of survival through songs, beginning in infancy by singing lullabies as they rocked their babies. One such song begins with loving tenderness and expresses gratitude for the precious child the singer has borne. In the second stanza, she cautions the child to be proud and to honor his parents in spite of the disadvantages of their lives:

FIGURE 15. *Rape*

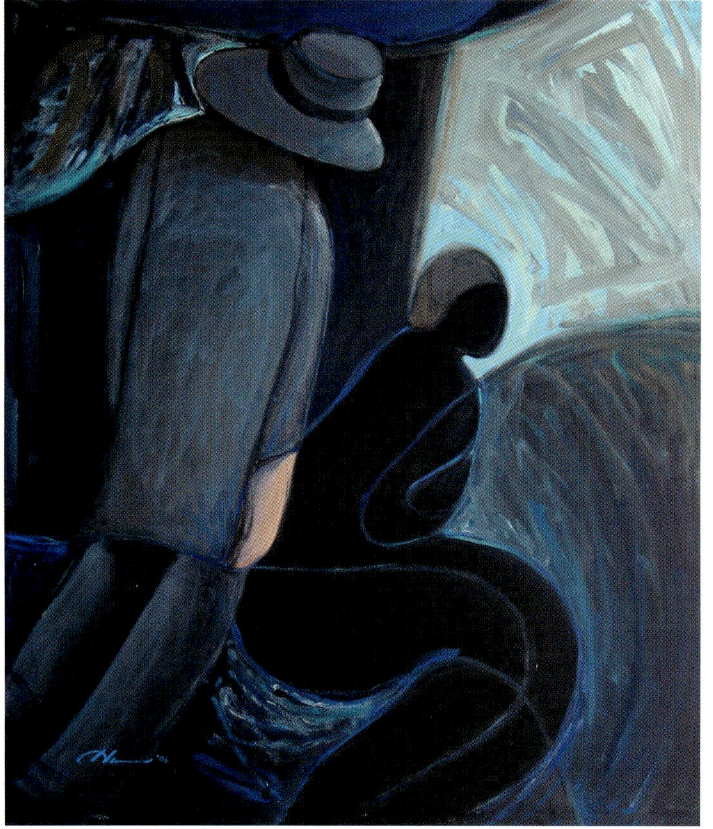

To a cabin in a woodland drear
You've come a mammy's heart to cheer,
In this ole slave cabin,
Your hands my heart strings grabbin',
Jes lay your head upon my bres,
An snuggle close an res and res,
My little colored chile.

Yo daddy ploughs ole massa's corn,
Yo mammy does the cooking,
She'll give dinner to her hungry chile
When nobody is a lookin'
Don't be ashamed my chile, I beg,
Ca[u]se you was hatched from a buzzard's egg;
My little colored chile.[12]

FIGURE 16. *Place of Respite*

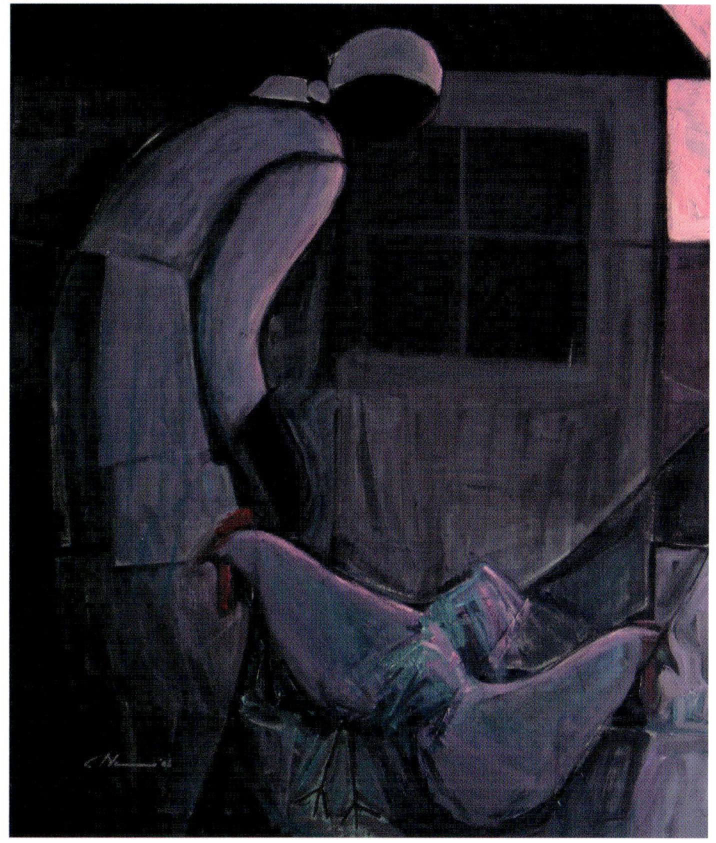

Many children born into slavery remembered in old age having been nurtured by their mothers. Lorenzo Ezell, interviewed in Beaumont, Texas, at age eighty-seven recalled, "Mamma was de good woman and I 'member her more dan once rockin' de little cradle and singin' to de baby."[13]

The conformation of the two figures in this painting also suggests a religious icon of the Madonna and Child. The background implies the light as it might be reflected on a mosaic panel. The ecclesiastic iconography is one that speaks to the thousands of bondsmen and bondswomen whose hearts could be lifted, if only briefly, by faith in a higher power. It brings attention to the role that religion and faith played in the lives of slaves. While black preachers taught the rudiments of Christianity and obedience to please their own white masters, there was always an underlying message of hope and relief from the brutalities of daily life on the plantation. Passages from the Bible described a beautiful life, an enchanting future—one with an absence of fear and a promise of joy. David West, a slave who escaped from King and Queen County, Virginia, dictated his story in 1856 and expressed his views of the Bible's lessons: "The Lord, He made us out of the dust of the earth, and He is the greatest Judge of the earth, yet even He does not compel us to serve Him: but among men, who are so frail, the stronger takes the weaker by force, and binds them slaves, and murders them."[14]

The slaves' primary environment for fostering family life, socializing, developing a cultural identity, and maintaining black solidarity, was "the quarter."[15] The workplace, where anonymity rendered them nearly invisible, was the secondary environment and far less important in determining personal associations. Holston's view of plantation housing for the slaves in *The Quarters* (figure 18) shows an eerily quiet and somber scene, devoid of people. The soft brown cabins are butted against one another, tightly connected by the weblike tangle of golden lunar beams, whose interlacing lines wrap around the whole community and reach up to "lasso" the moon. Its luminosity against the dark blue sky fills the upper half of the composition and calls to mind a guiding light through the darkness. Is it the close of a day over the quiet quarter? Is it a metaphor for the safety and security of the inhabitants?

FIGURE 17.
Madonna and Child

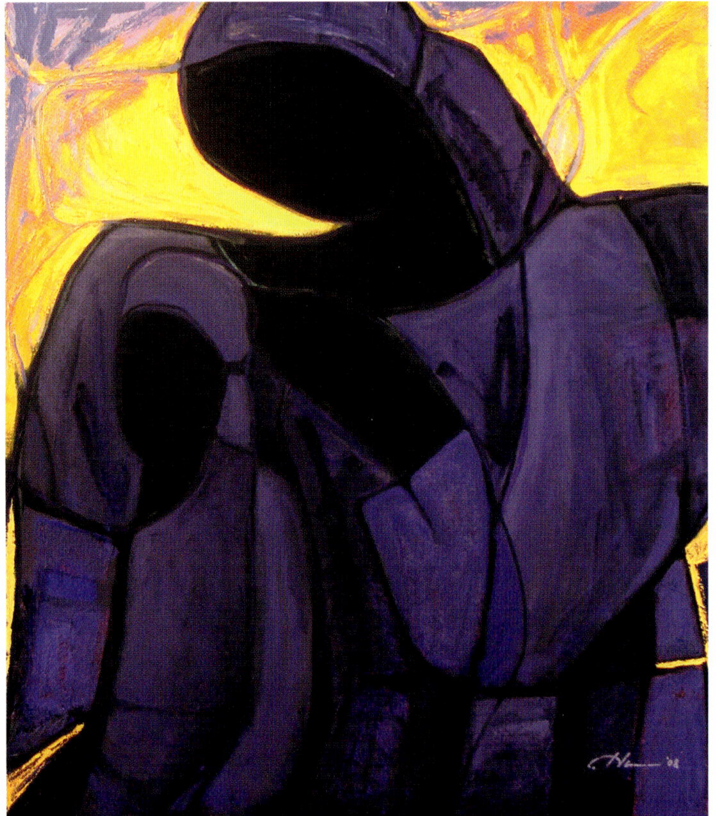

Holston's is not a literal depiction of slave quarters; rather, it is an interpretation that brings the viewer closer to the nuances of what it felt like to be there. The honesty and truth of this balanced arrangement contrasts sharply with the nineteenth-century artistic interpretation shown in Eastman Johnson's *Negro Life at the South* (figure 19).

Johnson's composition is a highly romanticized domestic scene of "happy" slaves at leisure in the yard of a dilapidated but spacious house. On the left there is a couple quietly talking, maybe flirting. The man in the middle is playing a banjo, while a woman on the right dances playfully with a child. Far to the right there is a young white woman in an elegant dress, perhaps the mistress, coming in through the gate to join the group in a surprise but seemingly welcome visit.[16] Can this cheerful family scene painted by a young, white, upper-class New England artist really give an accurate picture of slave life in 1855? The missing element here that is so prominently displayed in Holston's painting is the ominous atmosphere—the pervasive dread that characterized a slave's existence. Those who would have inhabited the quarter in Holston's interpretation would clearly not have enjoyed the casual banter and leisure time portrayed in Johnson's.

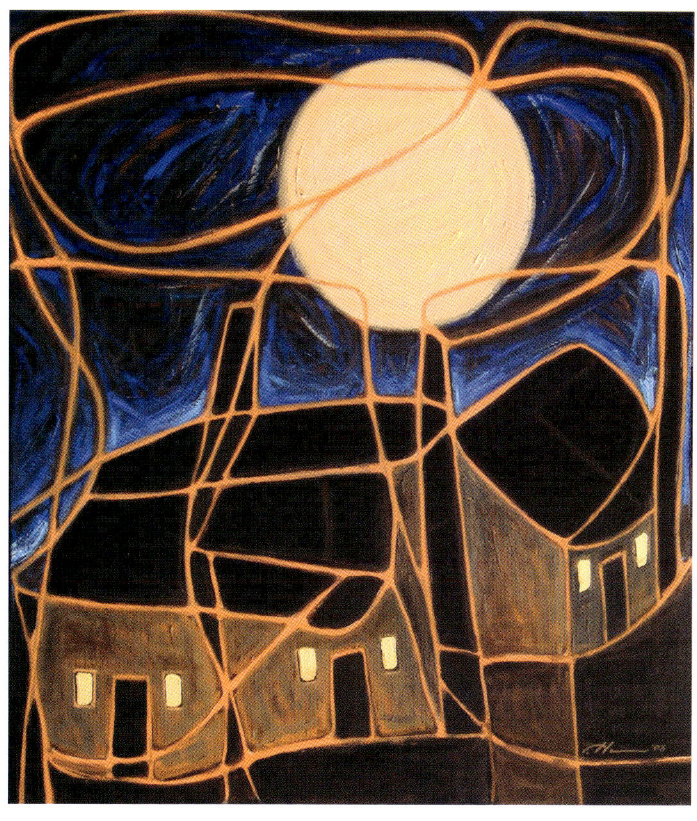

FIGURE 18. *The Quarters*

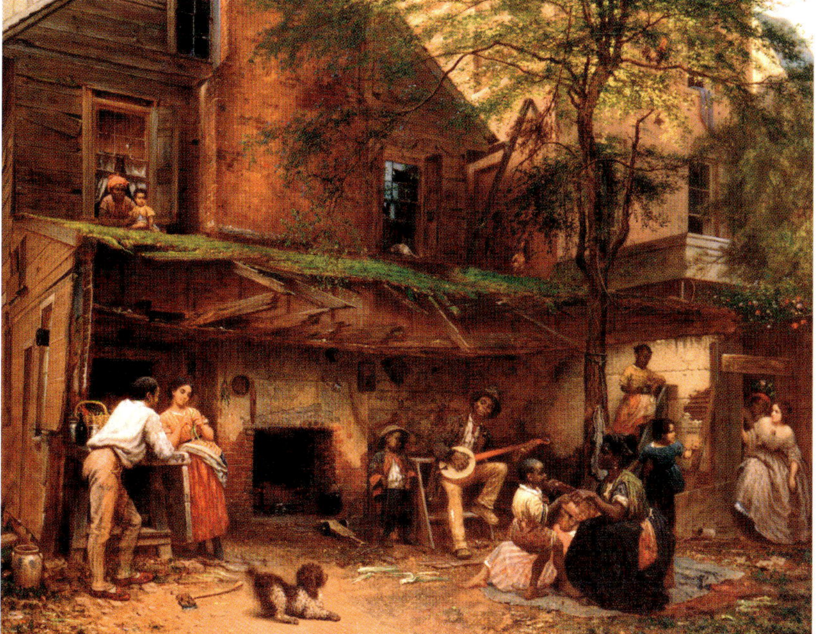

FIGURE 19. Eastman Johnson (American, 1824–1906). *Old Kentucky Home—Life in the South (Negro Life at the South),* 1859. Oil on canvas, 36 x 45¼ in. Collection of The New-York Historical Society; Robert L. Stuart Collection on permanent loan from The New York Public Library.

Notes

1. Benjamin Drew, *The Narratives of Fugitive Slaves* (Toronto: Prospero, 2000), 44. Mrs. Ellis, interviewed in 1855, escaped slavery at age thirty-two.
2. Ibid., 72.
3. Ibid., 43.
4. Henry Bibb, *The Life and Adventures of Henry Bibb, an American Slave,* with introduction by Charles J. Heglar (Madison: University of Wisconsin Press, 2000), 17. Originally published in 1849. After his initial escape to Canada in 1837, Henry Bibb (1815–1854) returned south several times to help family members escape. He was twice caught and sold back into slavery. By 1844 he was lecturing in public against slavery, following the example of Frederick Douglass and William Wells Brown. Bibb established Canada's first African American newspaper, the *Voice of the Fugitive,* in 1851.
5. James Oliver Horton and Lois E. Horton, *Slavery and the Making of America* (New York: Oxford University Press, 2005), 11.
6. Austin Steward, *Twenty-Two Years a Slave and Forty Years a Freeman* (Mineola, NY: Dover, 2004), 12. Originally published in 1857. Steward, after many failed attempts, escaped and settled in Rochester, New York, where he became a prosperous grocer. He was a founder of Wilberforce, a township in Canada.
7. Currently, *betimes* is used to indicate arrival before the usual or expected time—being early.
8. Bibb, *Life and Adventures of Henry Bibb,* 43.
9. Drew, *Narratives of Fugitive Slaves,* 54. George Johnson was interviewed within two hours of his arrival in St. Catharines, Canada, in 1855.
10. Bibb, *Life and Adventures of Henry Bibb,* 18.
11. Drew, *Narratives of Fugitive Slaves,* 38. Reverend Alexander Hemsley was interviewed at St. Catharines, a town in Canada with a home for refugee slaves. Hemsley, age unknown, was elderly and very ill, but was described by his interviewer as "a very intelligent man, and his face wears, notwithstanding his many trials . . . a remarkable expression of cheerfulness and good-will" (32).
12. John W. Blassingame, *The Slave Community: Plantation Life in the Antebellum South,* rev. ed. (New York: Oxford University Press, 1979), 183. Song originally published in Orland Kay Armstrong, ed., *Old Massa's People: The Old Slaves Tell Their Story,* 1931.
13. Norman R. Yetman, ed., *Voices from Slavery: 100 Authentic Slave Narratives* (Mineola, NY: Dover, 2000), 112.
14. Drew, *Narratives of Fugitive Slaves,* 91. David West left his wife and four children when his master died and he was certain he would be sold and separated from his family (87–88).
15. Blassingame, *Slave Community,* 105.
16. Eastman Johnson (1824–1906), intent on portraying American subjects, returned to the United States in 1855 from his studies abroad. In 1859 he made his first large genre painting, *Negro Life at the South (Old Kentucky Home—Life in the South),* depicting a house in the slave quarters of Washington, DC. Considered at the time to be his greatest masterpiece, this painting won him acclaim and election to the National Academy of Design in New York.

THE THIRD MOVEMENT

Journey of Escape

On my Underground Railroad I nebber run my train off de track and I nebber los' a passenger.

HARRIET TUBMAN[1]

It is in the third movement, *Journey of Escape,* that Holston reveals the most striking change of mood—one that progresses from acceptance and steadfast survival in bondage to the awakening notion of liberty. His compositions begin to evolve from contained, stationary forms to ones with a strong sense of moving forward. He expresses the hopefulness that we hear in the voices—voices no longer tacit, as quieted instruments, but of those who begin to vocalize the sounds of freedom. A young escapee from Kentucky was described as having "high notions of liberty prompting him to make repeated attempts to go to the state of Ohio or to some other part of the U.S. in which he would expect an unmolested enjoyment of freedom."[2] It is this kind of determination and persistence that inspired Holston to urge his figures to move and sway ever closer toward freedom. In this group of paintings, he discloses the burning desire for liberty that beats in the hearts of the enslaved, illuminating the dichotomy between the "absolute power of slavery and the human will to survive."[3] Holston uses deliberately articulated lines to judiciously arrange the forms, with a grace and finesse that is at once mysterious and liberating. The artistic interpretation is in human terms, the message is clear: Freedom was possible.

Escape was achievable for many because of the Underground Railroad, a developing system born to guide runaway slaves to a safe destination and finally to freedom in the North. Developed by individuals dedicated to the cause of freedom for the enslaved people of the South, this system relied on escape routes that, in both legend and fact, depended on courageous free blacks and sympathetic whites. Escapees traveled under dark of night, keeping to the woods or riverbanks, and secrecy was paramount—all associated with the escapes were sworn to it and pledged confidentiality. Most communication was verbal or with previously established signs and signals, and a clandestine language was created among the fugitives and those who aided in their escape. The "conductors" were those who escorted the fugitives along the "liberty lines" to the safe houses or "stations," driving wagons, steering boats, providing horses, or guiding them through the swamp and forest under the darkness of night. The "cargo" was the fugitive slaves. Three fugitives would be referred to, for example, as "three bales of black wool."[4]

The runaway slave who set out on such a journey demonstrated profound courage and bravery. John Parker, in an oral history, related his own as well as others' resolute determination: "This must be said for the slaves who took to the woods, they were above the average slave in intelligence and courage, otherwise they would never have started. Once they were started, no obstacle was too great for them to overcome."[5] He noted that most were strong and resourceful, as well as skilled in reading the landscape they would have to traverse.

Parker was one of many potentially responsible for the origin of the term *Underground Railroad*. He described how a frustrated slave owner, unable to find his vanished "property," remarked that he must have disappeared on an "underground road."[6] Many knew of the existence of this so-called railroad, but not all of these knew the term used to describe the network of sources and paths heading north. Lorenzo Ezell, a former slave, told his biogra-

FIGURE 20. Charles T. Webber (American, 1825–1911). *The Underground Railroad*, 1893. Oil on canvas, 52 3/16 x 76 1/8 in. (132.6 x 193.4 cm). Cincinnati Art Museum, Subscription Fund Purchase, 1927.26.

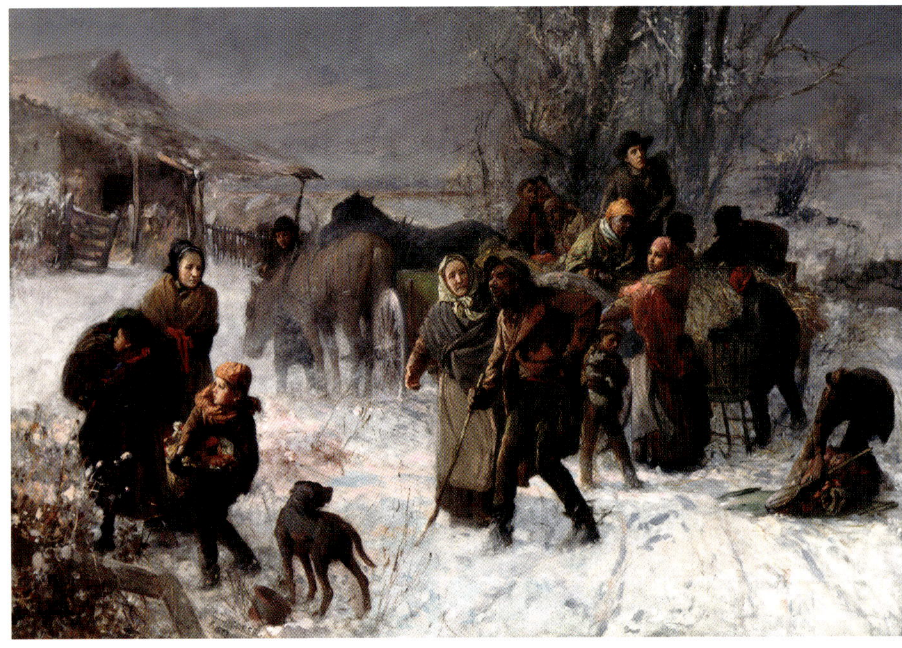

pher, "I saw dat place operated, though it wasn't knowed by dat den, but long time after I finds out dey call it part of de 'underground railroad.'"[7]

A well-known painting exhibited at the 1893 World's Fair in Chicago is largely responsible for the perception that prevails today of the abolitionists, Quakers, and freemen who, at their own peril, aided those in search of freedom. Thousands who attended the fair saw Charles T. Webber's painting *The Underground Railroad* (figure 20). It shows a dramatic and sympathetic picture of fugitives arriving at the home of Levi Coffin in Cincinnati.[8] The iconography illustrates the popular stereotype of the courageous Quaker conductors giving aid and comfort to the helpless, frightened slaves. The deeply moving subject and the emotional impact of the romantic style in which it is painted served for years to perpetuate this stereotype in place of the facts of the Underground Railroad and its supporters.

In *In Plain Sight* (figure 21) Holston portrays a scenario more likely than what appears in Webber's sentimental view. Here two figures are quietly and slowly moving forward in a carriage. Shielded by the dark of night and the protective canopy of their conveyance, they ride along anonymously, masquerading as a white passenger/owner with his black servant/driver. An account from 1891 says that escapees were "transferred from one abolitionist household to another . . . piloted by night through the woods, or concealed in farm wagons."[9] Secrecy and surreptitious activity were key to their success. Likewise, Holston's simple lines only subtly suggesting the figures in the carriage are key to the verisimilitude of this image. Convoluted complexity is not always necessary to convey truth and honesty, even when the subject is of grave importance.

FIGURE 21. *In Plain Sight*

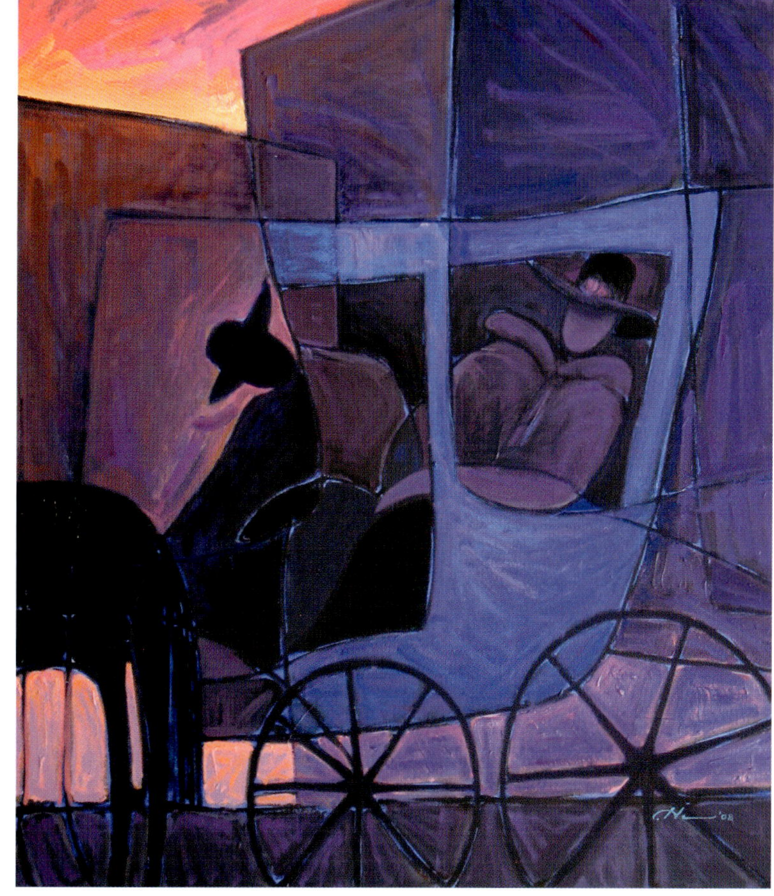

History has continued to describe the role of the abolitionists in romantic, legendary tones. But those who made the escape remember it very differently:

"The fugitive depended entirely on his own race for assistance," noted Parker.[10] Minister and former slave William Anderson dedicated his life to the freedom of others. "My two wagons, and carriage, and five horses were always at the command of the liberty-seeking fugitive."[11] Often assuming an active role in their own destiny, the enslaved were at the center of their own struggle for freedom, in the general tradition of refugees who emigrate to new lands to escape tyranny and oppression. Former slave John Lindsey recalled, "Finding that I was to get no assistance from any quarter, and that justice was refused me, I resolved to free myself."[12] Once they decided to take that bold step, they were not passive or at the complete mercy of others. The Underground Railroad system was intended to move silently through the night, calling no attention from authorities. The fear most slave owners had of an organized collective reprisal was unfounded. In contrast to heroic uprisings in the past that had often failed with considerable loss of life, individual escape was, for most, an example of nonviolent disobedience in response to unjust laws and customs.

FIGURE 22. Eastman Johnson (American, 1824–1906). *A Ride for Liberty—The Fugitive Slaves,* c. 1862. Oil on paper board, 21 15/16 x 26 1/8 in. (55.8 x 66.4 cm). Brooklyn Museum. 40.59a-b, Gift of Gwendolyn O.L. Conkling.

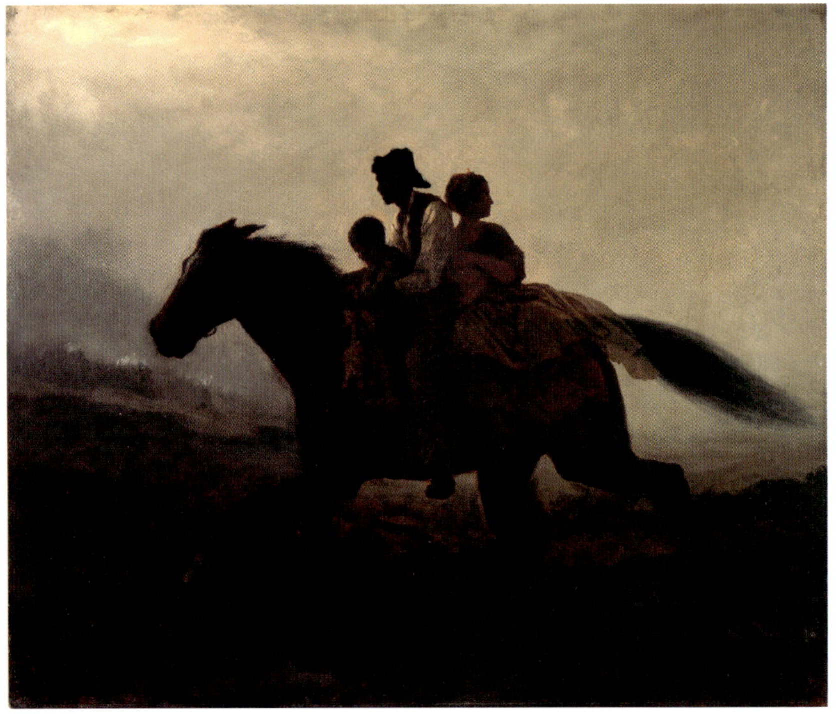

For many, the decision to run away was more reactive than planned, often forced by circumstances. David West recalled when his owner died: "I heard that I was to be sold, which would separate me from my family, and knowing no law which would defend me, I concluded to come away."[13] For some, like Parker, it was when the magnitude of oppression had reached the limits of tolerance: "I hated the injustices and restraints against my own initiative more than it is possible for words to express. To me that was the great curse of slavery."[14] Henry Banks recounted, "I ran away in order that master might sell me running . . . but I did not know where it was, nor how to get there. I stayed in the woods three months; I then thought I would start for a free country somewhere."[15]

Eastman Johnson continued to romanticize the plight of runaway slaves in his painting *A Ride for Liberty—The Fugitive Slaves,* c. 1862 (figure 22).[16] In this work a slave family of four rides into the wind on the back of a sturdy horse. Shielding his young son, the man looks earnestly ahead as the woman, holding a baby in her arms, keeps watch to the rear for any sign of pursuers. They are the heroes of their story, riding courageously and gallantly over an open field at twilight.

Holston sees a fugitive family as heroic in a different way, in a clearer light. *Freedom Stop* (figure 23) does not romanticize the bravery of its subjects, but a dauntless spirit is evident in it from the very act of their taking this dangerous step toward freedom. The clandestine nature of the scene gives a sense of realism in the context of Holston's abstract and painterly style. The couple, rendered in flat, broad planes of color, is silhouetted against a house that forms the background and allows them to blend into the environment of the village street. A mysterious billowing, red-orange form emanates from the roofline of the house and swoops out over the couple as if to shield them as they pass. They move quietly and keep a low profile, avoiding contact or notice. The muted colors suggest a soft twilight shadow around them, with the ever-present light appearing in the windows to guide them and keep hope in their hearts as they make their way soundlessly through the night.

FIGURE 23.
Freedom Stop

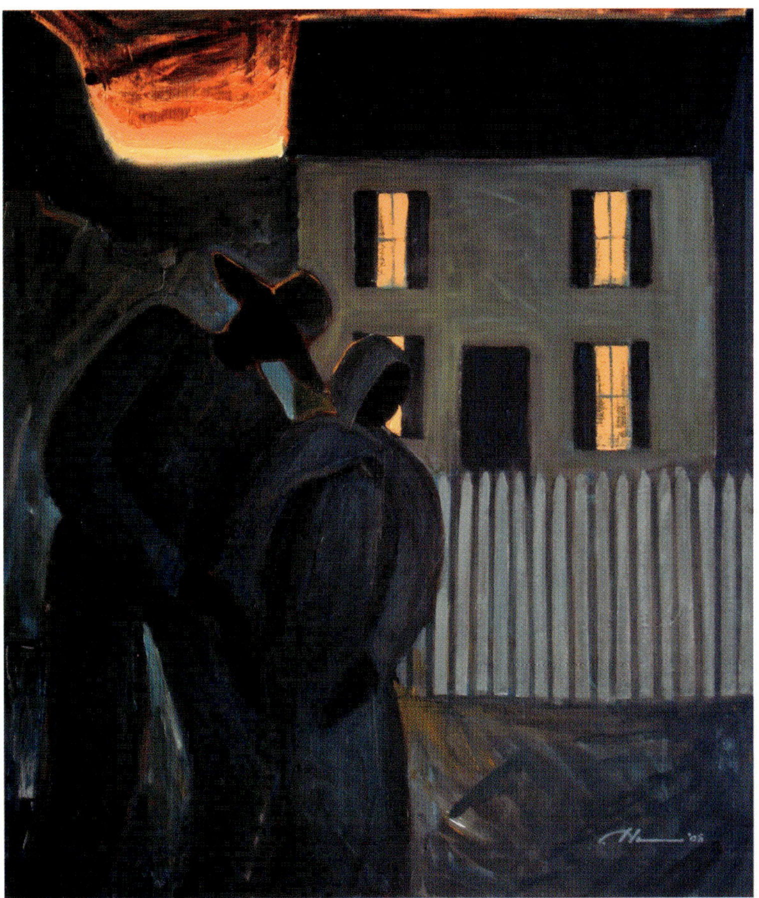

Often when slaves decided to set off on the path to freedom, they did not travel in groups, nor did they set out without direction or plan. Rather, many traveled alone and with clear determination. David West recalled, "When I left, I told my purpose to no one. I studied a plan by which I might get away, and I succeeded."[17] After long and thoughtful consideration, William Grose chose to follow his dream: "I picked up spunk, and said I would start. All this time, I dreamed on nights that I was getting clear. This put the notion into my head to start—a dream that I had reached a free soil and was perfectly safe."[18] Most had long known how to survive in the woods without sufficient provisions. While the territory beyond the boundaries of the plantation may have been unknown or uncharted, they knew how to read the stars and, most particularly, "every slave knew the north star led to freedom."[19] The act of leaving the plantation, taking that first step toward freedom, meant many more steps into danger and hardship as well as weeks or months spent in loneliness and fear. The risk was great, but the yearning for freedom outweighed the perilousness of the act.

Holston finds that moment in *The Long Road* (figure 24). In this painting he puts the group at a crossroads, contemplating their destiny. They stand hesitantly in the lower right of the composition, with a winding road rising and swirling behind them. The road, a deep violet ribbon of color, wraps around the vertical trees to the left. These stand straight and tall like a fettered colonnade, blocking the past from the future that lies ahead. It is as if the barrier between bondage and freedom is in bondage itself. The mood is one of profound silence, expressed by a stillness in which the figures stop and listen, mindful of the quiet. The man holds the others close as he contemplates his responsibility for their safety. It is but a momentary stop, just as a musician expresses a full, concluding rest, a quiet pause between two segments of high volume.[20] Holston leaves no doubt about their decision. The bold curving and lyrical lines emerge, seeming to reach for the group, hovering above them protectively and urging them forward. As they move away from the road and the sanctuary of the woods, they are momentarily exposed, both literally and figuratively. What will be next for them? The risks are great, but the inherent yearning for freedom cannot be denied. A popular African American spiritual informed and prepared people for the arduous conditions such as Holston envisions. The lyrics also offered hope for a better place beyond:

FIGURE 24.
The Long Road

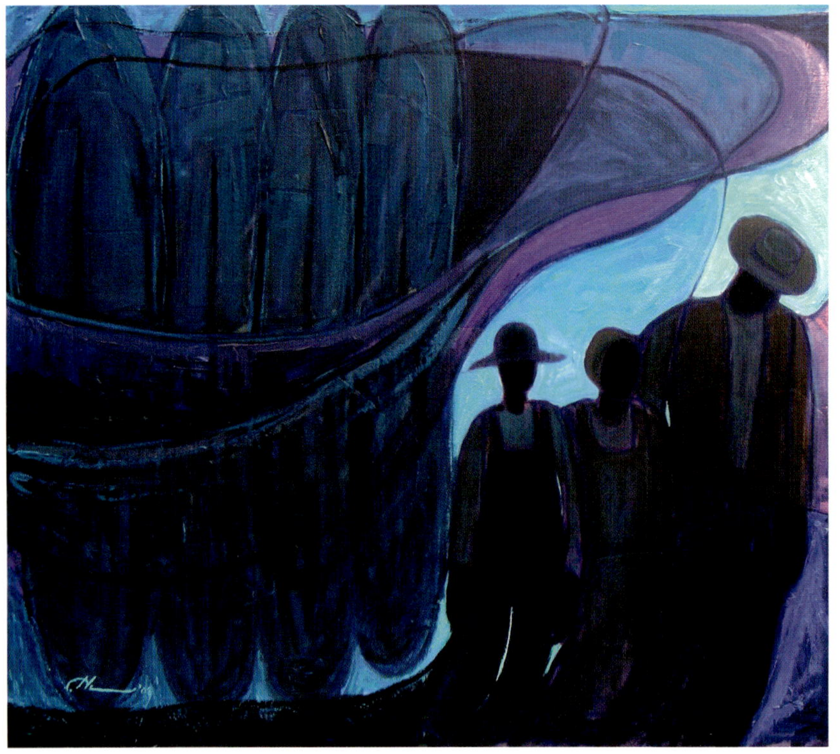

Dark and thorny is the pathway,
Where the pilgrim makes his way;
But beyond this vale of sorrow,
Lie the fields of endless days.[21]

In *Promising Portal* (figure 25), Holston gives a view deep into the ominous forest that was often the first encounter on the journey. There is a stark contrast between the hopeful light shining through the trees and the dark brown of the tree trunks themselves—trees through which the fugitives must make their way into the void of space beyond. The broad, sweeping canopy of the trees dominates the upper area of the composition, providing concealment and safety for those in the forest. The wide swirling lines expand the feeling of motion as they vibrate against one another like the strident notes of a trumpet.

Wooded areas did not ensure protection for travelers. Fugitives were always aware of the pursuit of the patrollers, referred to in the slave vernacular as "patter rollers."[22] These were the bounty hunters or slave catchers who made their living hunting runaways for the reward offered by slave owners. Slaves sang, "Patter-roll around me. Thank God he no ketch me,"[23] to warn others when a patroller was present in the field. Former slaves remembered the fear instilled by the inevitable consequences of a dreaded encounter: "The patter rollers would get us . . . sometimes [they] hit us just to hear us holler."[24] Holston's large, menacing figure in *Patter-Roller* (figure 26) has his gun ready and his dog on the scent. The light of the moon does not reflect its glow on him or his dog; rather, it remains a beacon reserved for the hunted, not the hunter. The round moon, centered in a swirling lunar atmosphere, mimics the shape of the patroller's hat, both brim and crown, as he leans his head away from the intense light. He is focused on his

FIGURE 25.
Promising Portal

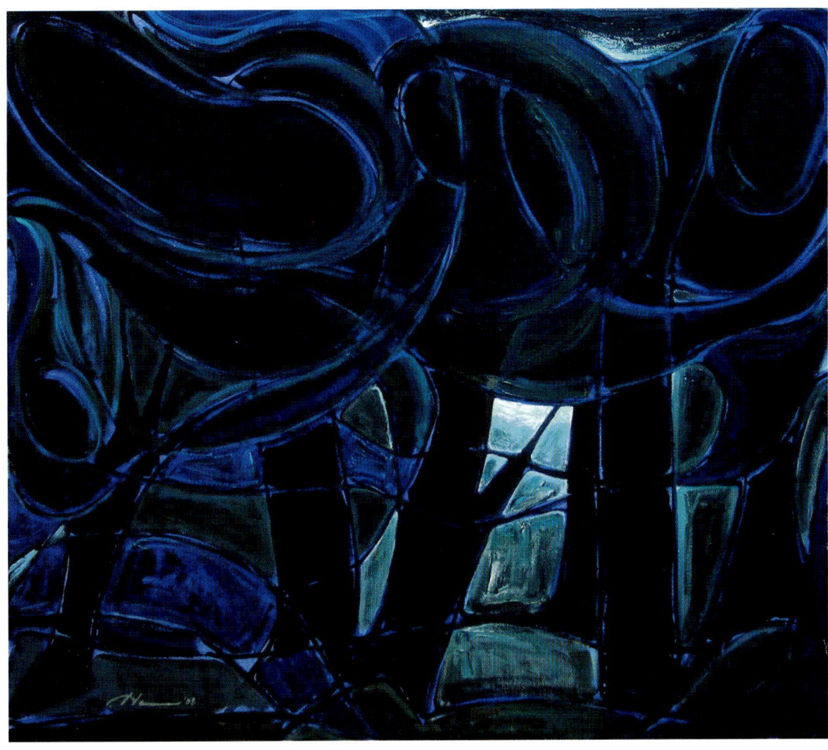

own sinister intent. The symbolism may attest to the fact that fugitives often eluded capture because of their ingenuity and undaunted bravery. Isaac Williams remembered, "Runaways knew . . . they could keep clear of the hounds by rubbing the soles of their shoes with red onion or spruce pine."[25]

Scholars have studied many legendary tales of slave hunters being outsmarted by the abolitionists in the Underground Railroad system.[26] These tales usually involve imaginative hiding places, called "hidey-holes,"[27] as well as secret codes and word-of-mouth communication, called "underground grape-vine dispatches."[28]

As the journey continued, the fugitive took care to remain anonymous, whether assistance came from a well-known abolitionist or from a chance exchange with a helpful stranger. Walt Whitman wrote of his encounter with a fugitive in poetic verse and yet never revealed his identity nor professed any curiosity about his "guest":

FIGURE 26.
Patter-Roller

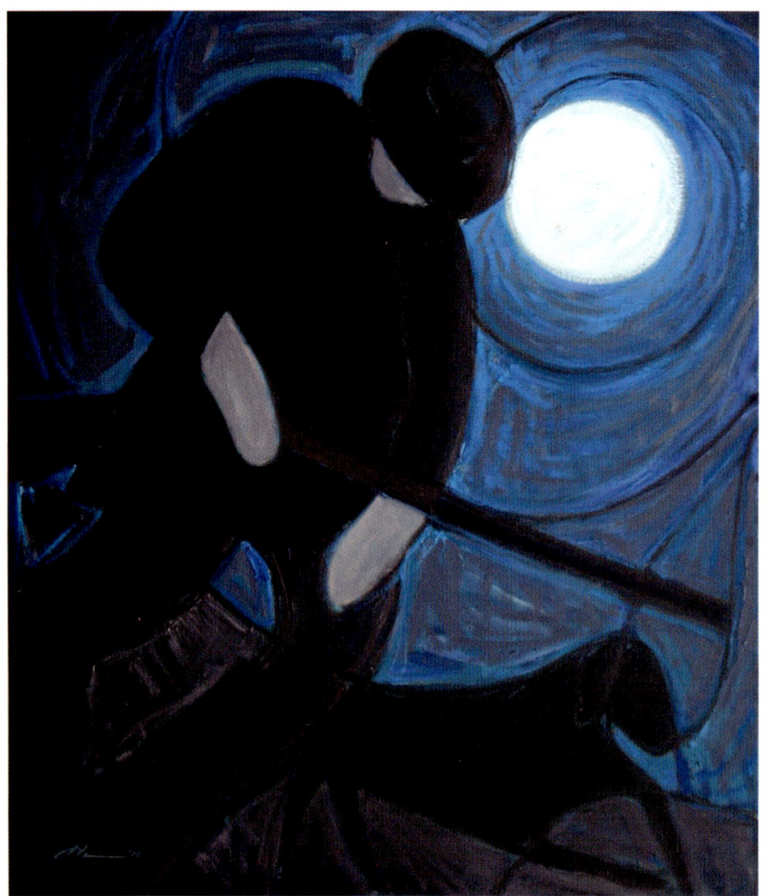

The runaway slave came to my
house and stopped outside,
I heard his motions crackling the
twigs of the woodpile, . . .
And gave him a room . . . and gave
him some coarse clean clothes, . . .
He staid with me a week before he
was recuperated and passed north,
I had him sit next me at table . . .
my firelock leaned in the corner.[29]

The anonymity shown in *Spectre of the Hunt* (figure 27) could very well be the kind of encounter Whitman describes. Barely distinguishable in the darkness of night, the silhouettes of the figures can be seen within a barnyard. One is seated, leaning forward, spent with exhaustion and clearly in need of rest. The young boy in the foreground is rendered in simple, flat planes of color against a dark and foreboding background. He is frozen in fear as he faces the vision, real or imagined, of a vicious, oversized dog looming menacingly above him. Is the seated figure unaware of the threat the boy perceives? Is this a testimony to the psychological stress that slave children fleeing with fugitive parents felt when faced with danger beyond comprehension? The many levels of emotion and anxiety are echoed in the layers of color and the palpable texture within this painting.

The body of work in this movement celebrates the courage and heroism of those who made the journey of escape. For those who were successful in reaching their goal, the world would be a very different place.

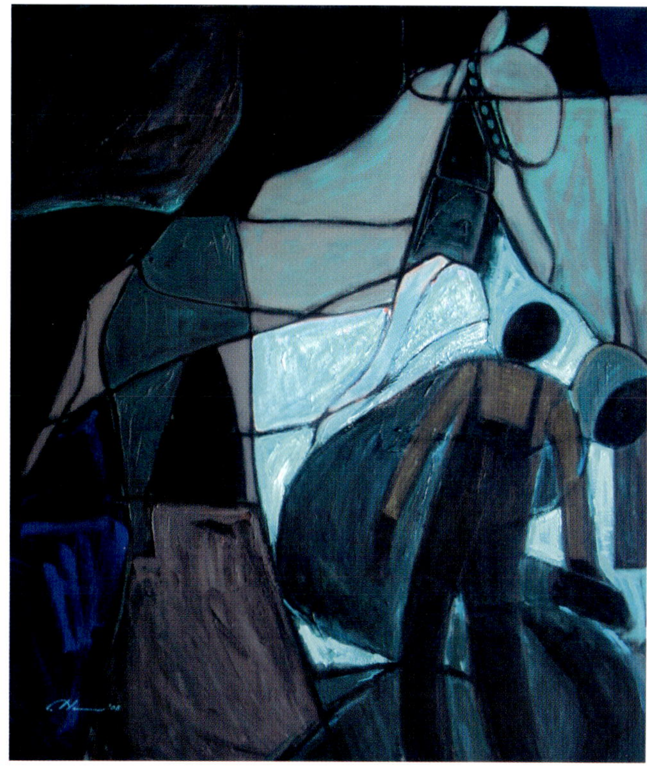

FIGURE 27. *Spectre of the Hunt*

Notes

1. Catherine Clinton, *Harriet Tubman: The Road to Freedom* (New York: Little, Brown & Co., 2004), 216. Quote engraved on a bronze tablet installed on the Tubman Home in Auburn, New York. The use of dialect on the plaque has been questioned, particularly the authenticity of her manner of speech.
2. John Hope Franklin and Loren Schweninger, *Runaway Slaves: Rebels on the Plantation* (New York: Oxford University Press, 1999), 116. William Henry Thomas, a sixteen-year-old fugitive who escaped through the Allegheny Mountains, was caught in Kentucky in 1821 and escaped a second time with a successful crossing of the Ohio River.
3. David Blight, ed., *Passages to Freedom: The Underground Railroad in History and Memory* (New York: Smithsonian Books/HarperCollins, in association with the National Underground Railroad Freedom Center, 2004), 7.
4. Clinton, *Harriet Tubman,* 37.
5. John Parker, *His Promised Land: The Autobiography of John P. Parker, Former Slave and Conductor on the Underground Railroad,* ed. Stuart Sprague (New York: Norton, 1996), 25. Parker dictated his history to Frank Moody Gregg; the original manuscript is in the Rankin/Parker collection at Duke University. John P. Parker (1827–1900), a former slave, bought his freedom in 1845 and moved to Ripley, Ohio, where he became a conductor and stationmaster for the Underground Railroad. Frank Moody Gregg was a journalist for the *Chattanooga News,* doing a story on the woman who inspired the Eliza character in Harriet Beecher Stowe's *Uncle Tom's Cabin* (1852), when he met Parker. Parker may have been among those who saw "Eliza," the woman who came to John Rankin's house after forging the frozen Ohio River with her child in her arms, an event recounted in

Stowe's book. John Rankin (1793–1886), a Presbyterian minister, educator, and abolitionist, became known as one of Ohio's first and most active conductors. His Ripley home was a frequented "station" along the Underground Railroad. In 2007 John P. Parker was the subject of a fully staged opera, *Rise for Freedom,* scored for a seventeen-piece chamber orchestra and commissioned by Cincinnati Opera.

6. Ibid., 9. This is only one of many versions of the story. With little documented evidence, most theories come from oral histories or unsubstantiated diary entries. See also note 19 below.
7. Norman R. Yetman, ed., *Voices from Slavery: 100 Authentic Slave Narratives* (Mineola, NY: Dover, 2000), 111. Lorenzo Ezell was interviewed in Beaumont, Texas, at age eighty-seven.
8. Larry Gara, *The Liberty Line: The Legend of the Underground Railroad* (Lexington: University Press of Kentucky, 1961), 1; Blight, *Passages to Freedom,* 236–237. Charles T. Webber (1825–1911), portrait, history, and landscape painter, was a leader in Cincinnati art circles during the latter half of the nineteenth century. He received wide acclaim for this painting. Levi Coffin (1798–1877), a Quaker and an abolitionist, has been referred to as the "President of the Underground Railroad," the title allegedly coming from a slave catcher who said, "There's an underground railroad going on here, and Levi's the president of it." Coffin claimed to have been involved in the escape of about three thousand slaves.
9. Ibid., 15.
10. Parker, *His Promised Land,* 137.
11. Keith P. Griffler, *Front Line of Freedom: African Americans and the Forging of the Underground Railroad in the Ohio Valley* (Lexington: University Press of Kentucky, 2004), 47. William Anderson escaped to freedom in 1836 and became a central operative in the Underground Railroad.
12. Benjamin Drew, *The Narratives of Fugitive Slaves* (Toronto: Prospero, 2000), 77. John W. Lindsey, born to free black parents, was abducted into slavery and later escaped from Tennessee to Canada entirely destitute. When he provided his oral history to Benjamin Drew in 1856, he was reputed to be worth approximately $10,000, a near fortune at that time.
13. Ibid., 88. See also note 14, p. 36.
14. Parker, *His Promised Land,* 70.
15. Drew, *Narratives of Fugitive Slaves,* 75. Henry Banks was born in 1835 in Virginia and escaped in his early twenties. To sell or buy someone "running" was a common practice among slave hunters (34). They would buy the "rights" to an escaped slave from his or her owner for a low price; then, if they could catch the fugitive, they would sell him or her for full market value, profiting from the difference.
16. The scene is purported to be based on an incident that Johnson witnessed during the Civil War battle of Manassas (according to *Africans in America,* a four-part series on "America's journey through slavery" produced by PBS and summarized on its website: http://www.pbs.org/wgbh/aia/home.html).
17. Drew, *Narratives of Fugitive Slaves,* 88.
18. Ibid., 85. William Grose, a slave at Harpers Ferry, Virginia, was twenty-five years old when, after several unsuccessful attempts, he made his escape to Canada in 1851.
19. Parker, *His Promised Land,* 71. Clinton, *Harriet Tubman,* discusses how Harriet Tubman relied on the North Star to find her way (34). Ann Hagedorn, *Beyond the River: The Untold Story of the Heroes of the Underground Railroad* (New York: Simon & Schuster, 2002), notes the legend of slaves learning from a sailor to follow the North Star and to sing the drinking song "The Drinking Gourd" ("Follow the drinking gourd . . .") (39). The Drinking Gourd was another name for the Big Dipper, which helped them locate the North Star.
20. Lawrence Haward, *Music in Painting* (New York: Pitman, 1948), 35.
21. Clinton, *Harriet Tubman,* 39. Originally published in 1886, in Sarah H. Bradford, *Harriet Tubman: The Moses of Her People.*
22. Gara, *Liberty Line,* 2.
23. James Oliver Horton and Lois E. Horton, *Slavery and the Making of America* (New York: Oxford University Press, 2005), 125.
24. Yetman, *Voices from Slavery,* 92. Elige Davison was interviewed in Madisonville, Texas, at age eighty-six.
25. Drew, *Narratives of Fugitive Slaves,* 64.
26. Gara, *Liberty Line,* 12. Gara mentions two historians whose seminal works repeat some of the legends. These are Henrietta Buckmaster, *Let My People Go: The Story of the Underground Railroad and the Growth of the Abolition Movement* (1959), and William Breyfogle, *Make Free: The Story of the Underground Railroad* (1958).
27. Karolyn Smardz Frost, *I've Got a Home in Glory Land: A Lost Tale of the Underground Railroad* (New York: Farrar, Straus and Giroux, 2007), 42.
28. Gara, *Liberty Line,* 12.
29. Walt Whitman, *The Portable Walt Whitman,* ed. Mark Van Doren (Viking, 1945, 1973), 41. Excerpt from "Song of Myself," originally published in 1855. Walt Whitman (1819–1892) was an American poet, essayist, and humanist.

THE FOURTH MOVEMENT

Color in Freedom

We were at times remarkably buoyant, singing hymns, and making joyous exclamations . . .

"O Canaan, sweet Canaan

I am bound for the land of Canaan . . ."

We meant to reach the North, and the North was our Canaan.

FREDERICK DOUGLASS[1]

The fourth movement in the exhibition, *Color in Freedom,* is where Holston's palette bursts into a vivid complement of colors representing the elation that springs from success. The joy and exuberance expressed in this body of work will entice the viewer to feel the emotion and drama of each celebratory moment portrayed. A colorful orchestral crescendo erupts within each painting, reaching its highest pitch in bold lines and brilliant luminosity. The joy of freedom and justice cannot be denied.

It was not only the formerly enslaved who would benefit from their freedom; the concept would bring an optimism and hopefulness to the moral consciousness of all Americans. Many abolitionist pamphlets and flyers suggested that slavery was not only destructive to those in bondage, but also a menace to the rights of all Americans.[2] Henry David Thoreau, writing at a time when the issue of slavery was tearing the young nation apart, wrote passionately about the effect slavery had on the new democracy and expressed the urgent need to abolish it. His message of "synergy and freedom" stressed that a slave owner could never be free or enjoy true liberty if he remained committed to the institution of forced slavery. "What is the value of any political freedom," he wrote, "but as a means to moral freedom?"[3] Recited on New Year's Day 1863 at the Boston Music Hall, Ralph Waldo Emerson's epic poem "Boston Hymn"—a salute to Lincoln's Emancipation Proclamation—pointed out the value that emancipation brought to the whole country:

Today unbind the captive,
So only are ye unbound;
Lift up a people from the dust,
Trump of their rescue, sound!

Pay ransom to the owner,
And fill the bag to the brim.
Who is the owner? The slave is owner,
And ever was. Pay him.[4]

Holston expresses these lofty ideals in his color-filled compositions. The influence of the light—seen both boldly luminous and softly flickering throughout the paintings that guided us through the previous three movements—is coming to fruition. In *Sun Warms the Freemen* (figure 28), the light bursts forth to embrace the sensations associated with Synchromism; Holston combines color intensity with overlapping lines to reflect the drama and tension of the iconography. The work expresses a joyousness, liberally compounded with cautious optimism, that attends the glory of freedom.

FIGURE 28.
Sun Warms the Freemen

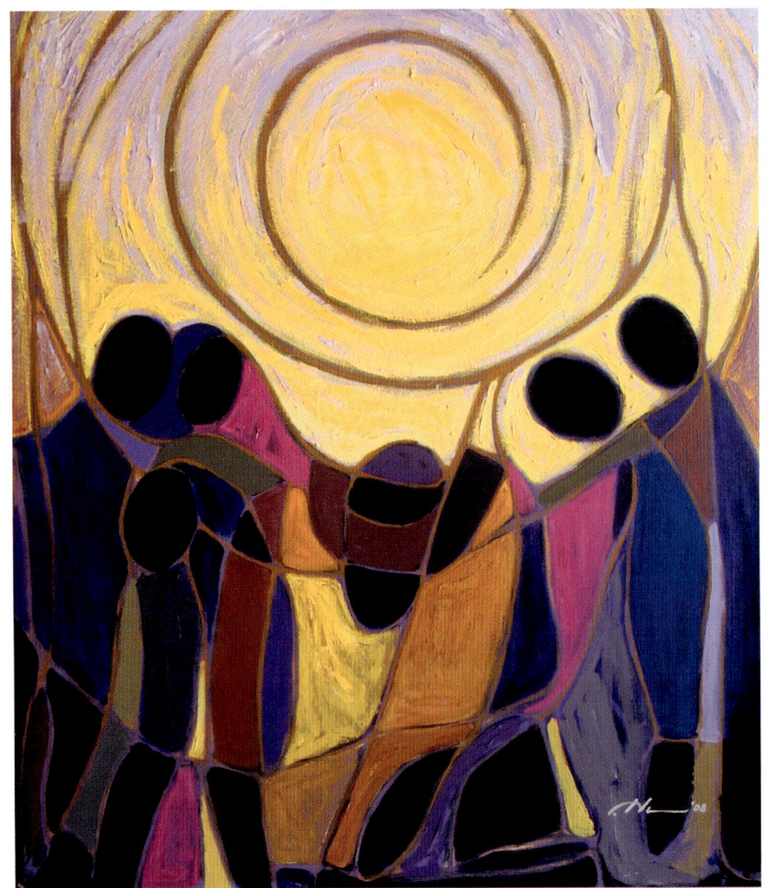

Here Holston opens the sky to an expanded sphere of the sun. The banded lines rotate in even circles of extended light, stretching to the edges of the canvas and reaching to encircle the group below. We began the journey in the first movement with an image of enslaved Africans closely chained together but turning away from one another (figure 10). In *Sun Warms the Freemen,* Holston once again depicts the figures in a tightly enclosed space to make them appear as a solid, single form. But in this painting, there is solidarity among the figures as they respectfully acknowledge one another. The disproportionate size of the figure in the center could suggest a hierarchal importance, but this theory belies the humility and humble gesture of the bowed head, indicating one who reluctantly accepts a leadership role. There is no arrogant power or authority implied, but rather the strength necessary to bring liberty to those who would follow. John Parker acknowledged, "These long distance travelers were usually strong physically, as well as people of character, and were resourceful when confronted with trouble, otherwise they could have never escaped."[5]

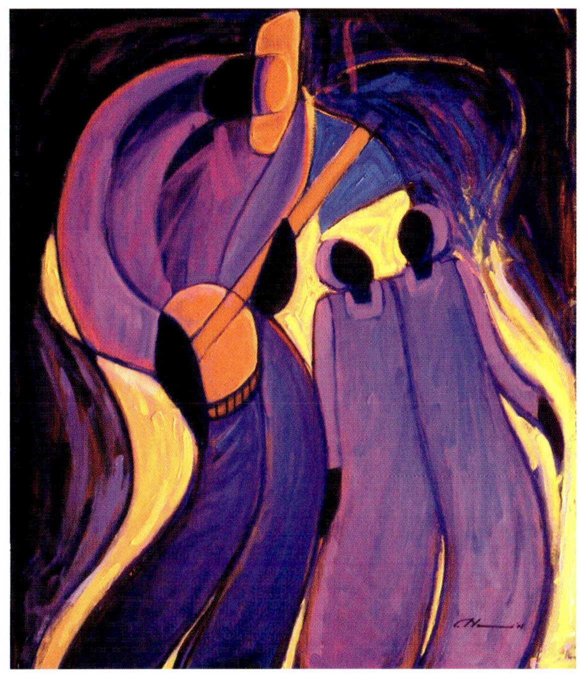

FIGURE 29. *Rhythm of Renewal*

In *Rhythm of Renewal* (figure 29), Holston puts the musician in a towering position, leaning over the girls, who listen closely to his melody. The gentle *contrapposto* curve of his body does not, however, display dominance or superiority; rather, his is a protective presence. His body, serpentine along the left side of the composition, leads the eye to the curved trajectory of the line above the heads of the girls—a line that seems to connect a mutual sense of peace among them. The musician remains focused on his instrument, seeming intent on providing a musical inspiration worthy of the importance of the event—the first precious notes of freedom. Sunlight bathes the composition, shining brightly above and reflecting on the figures who move back and forth to the music.

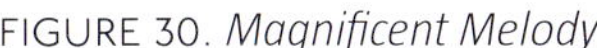

FIGURE 30. *Magnificent Melody*

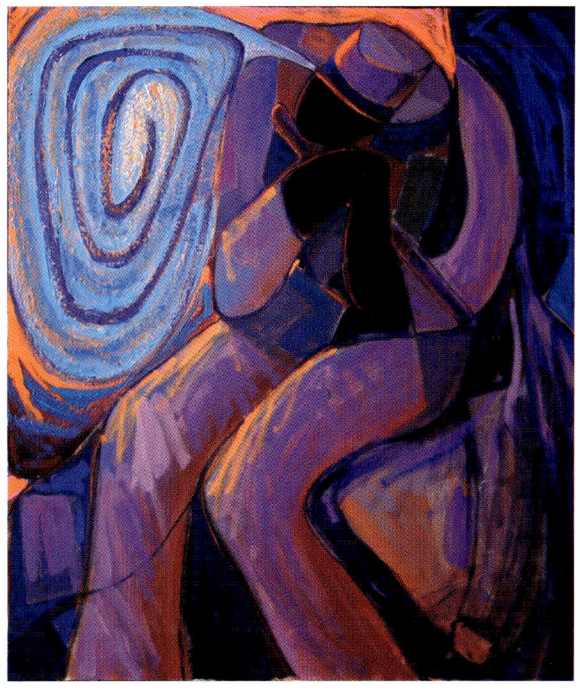

Holston explores the varied responses people felt when freedom was achieved. Some express their feelings in quiet introspection and solitude, and *Magnificent Melody* (figure 30) is just such an example. The lone figure is shown swaying to his own inner rhythm, playing his song as a solo. The lines on the left are rendered in soft, melancholy colors meandering in concentric circles. The color echoes around the canvas, absorbing the figure and providing a temporary refuge. Holston draws attention to the strong, steady hands as they cradle his face, setting it at a pensive angle. He is rendered in simple curvilinear lines that divide the canvas diagonally in the center. The figure is subdued and contemplative, as if realizing a newfound self-worth—an example, perhaps, of thoughts described by former slave William Grose: "I served twenty-five years in slavery, and about five I have been free. I feel now like a man, while before I felt more as though I were but a brute."[6] Holston's figure could, perhaps, be reflecting on the past, where he has been, and looking to the future, where he is going. Austin Steward recognized that with freedom comes responsibility: "[T]he colored man has yet a prominent part to act in this highly-favored Republic,—of what description the future must determine."[7] As was the case with many, he must realize it is not only his body that is free, but also his mind and soul. Reverend Alexander Hemsley expressed such thoughts to his biographer: "My idea of freedom . . . was a state of liberty for the mind . . . there was a freedom of thought, which I could not enjoy unless I were free."[8]

Holston produced *Jubilation* (figure 31) with a few simple but dynamic lines and vibrant colors juxtaposed to enhance the intensity of the mood. He captures the awakening movement of those who are slowly realizing the triumph of their journey and building an enthusiasm that will transform contemplation to exuberant expression. They begin to sway, slowly and deliberately, each figure moving in concert with the others. This work brings attention to the rejoicing and singing that will soon resonate for those who have shed their shackles and broken free of the lash. They can allow themselves to recognize the fulfillment of their dream, to appreciate a newfound purpose, and to anticipate the true meaning of personal and collective freedom. To be free meant more than to turn away from bondage. To take charge of one's own life, at great peril, meant owning oneself, "giving oneself a full measure of autonomy."[9]

FIGURE 31. *Jubilation*

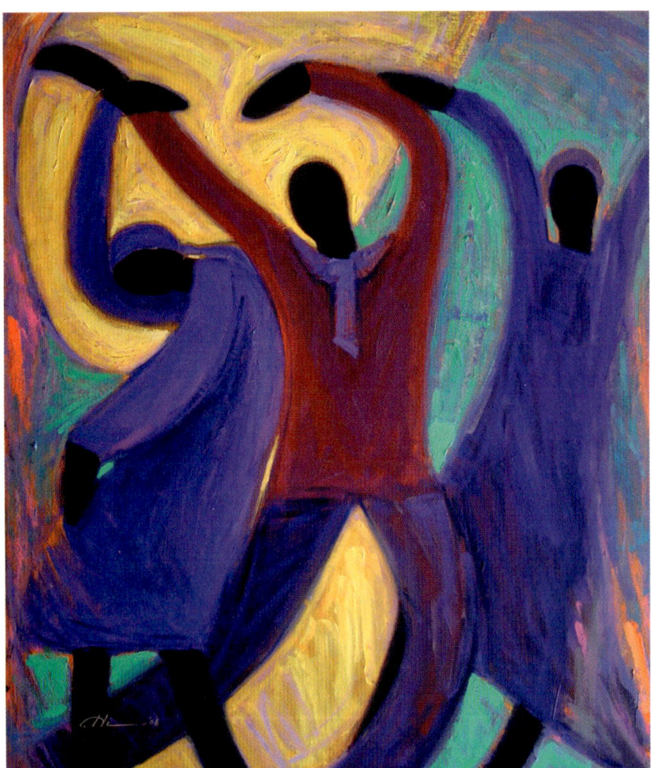

With the promise of freedom came the realization of responsibility. Holston reminds us in *Freedom Realized* (figure 32) just how sobering and serious the task of creating new lives and assuming leadership roles within the new community would be. This painting briefly interrupts the celebratory mood with a more solemn iconography. Here the young people are contemplative as they collectively move toward the strong light that has guided them to this moment, a light that surrounds them with optimism. There is no hesitation or fear suggested here; rather, they stand together, tall and square-shouldered, willing and resolute, confident and hopeful. The diptych, two canvases seen as one continuous scene, suggests a connecting of formerly separated lives—new beginnings, new generations, new families, new alliances, and success for the future.

In Holston's *Righteous Rejoicing* (figure 33), the sensation of movement is clear in the interplay of colors revolving with and interlacing one another around the sun in the upper part of the canvas. The motion is intensified by the figures below, who move in and out of focus as they reach toward the light. This light is rendered in color tones that echo the rhythmic beating of a drum or the reverberating sound of a banjo; the pitch is associated with the exhilaration of emotion. Unable and disinclined to contain the exuberance any longer, the whole painting explodes with jubilant dancing under the brilliant, iridescent sky—a sky centrally focused on the ever-present sun that has been a ray of light and hope from the beginning of the pilgrimage north. Holston depicts the figures singing in a chorus, dancing in unison, and rejoicing in the euphoria of the moment.

FIGURE 32.
Freedom Realized (Diptych)

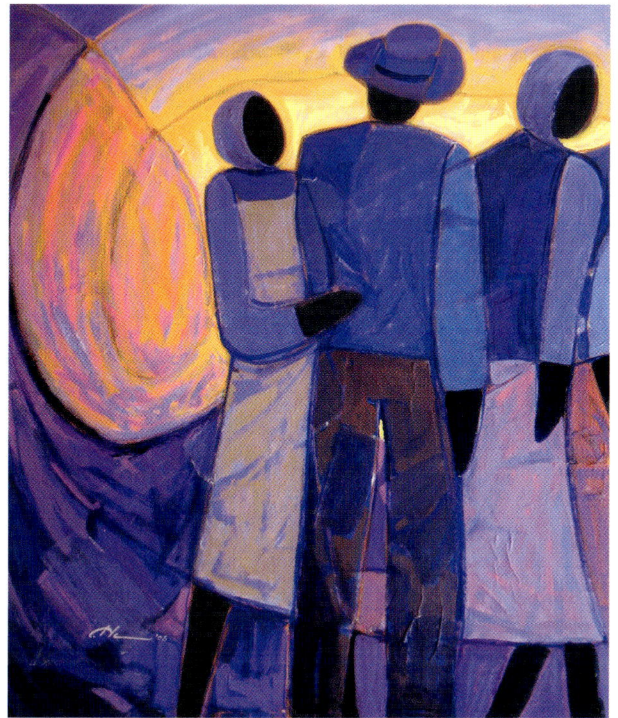

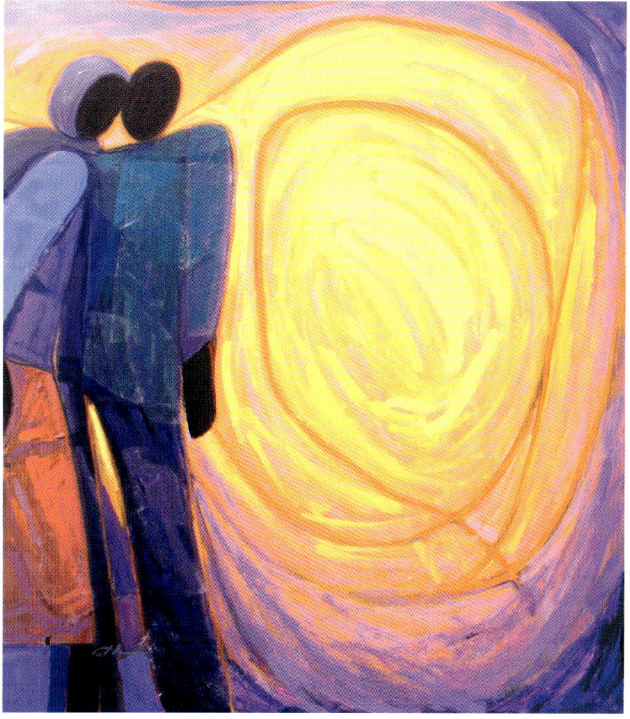

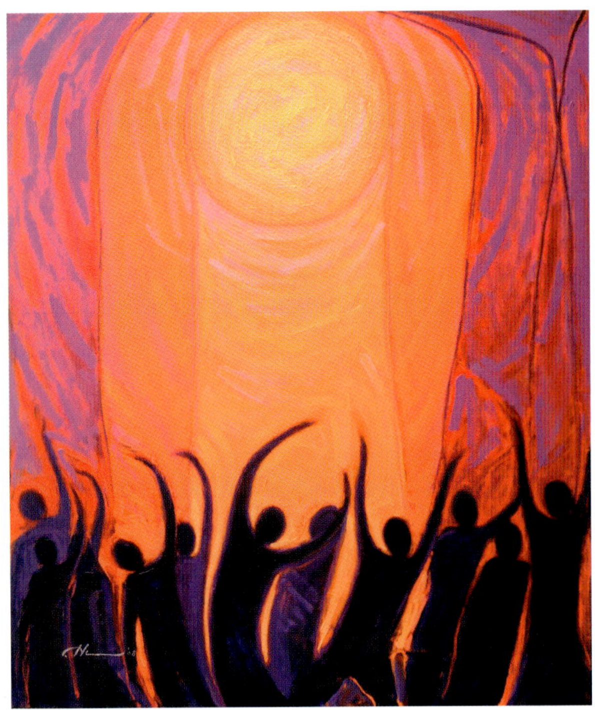

Freedom brought an openness and merriment that few had known in their lifetime. This work expresses the joy of being alive, of uninhibited happiness—of being free.

FIGURE 33. *Righteous Rejoicing*

Notes

1. Fergus Bordewich, *Bound for Canaan: The Underground Railroad and the War for the Soul of America* (New York: Amistad, 2005). According to Douglass, black spirituals were as much about a hope for freedom as they were about religious salvation.
2. David Hackett Fischer, *Liberty and Freedom: A Visual History of America's Founding Ideas* (New York: Oxford University Press, 2004), 280. The Fugitive Slave Act of 1850 prompted wide discussion of the effects of slavery on the population at large.
3. Henry David Thoreau, *The Journal of Henry David Thoreau* (Boston: Houghton Mifflin, 1906), quoted in Fischer, *Liberty and Freedom,* 259. Henry David Thoreau (1817–1862) was a naturalist, transcendentalist, philosopher, critic, and lifelong abolitionist. His philosophy of nonviolent resistance has long been considered an inspiration to later figures such as Mohandas Gandhi and Martin Luther King Jr.
4. Carlos Baker, *Emerson Among the Eccentrics: A Group Portrait* (New York: Penguin, 1996), 440. Ralph Waldo Emerson (1803–1882) was a noted abolitionist, philosopher, and orator, and a founder of Transcendentalism.
5. John Parker, *His Promised Land: The Autobiography of John P. Parker, Former Slave and Conductor on the Underground Railroad,* ed. Stuart Sprague (New York: Norton, 1996), 138.
6. Benjamin Drew, *The Narratives of Fugitive Slaves* (Toronto: Prospero, 2000), 86. See also note 18, p. 46.
7. Austin Steward, *Twenty-Two Years a Slave and Forty Years a Freeman* (Mineola, NY: Dover, 2004), 140. See also note 20, p. 46.
8. Drew, *Narratives of Fugitive Slaves,* 33. See also note 11, p. 36.
9. Beverly Lowry, *Harriet Tubman: Imagining a Life* (New York: Doubleday, 2007), 164.

Select Bibliography

HISTORY

Appleby, Joyce. *Inheriting the Revolution: The First Generation of Americans*. Cambridge, MA: Harvard University Press, 2000.

Berlin, Ira. *Generations of Captivity: A History of African-American Slaves*. Cambridge, MA: Harvard University Press, 2003.

Blassingame, John W. *The Slave Community: Plantation Life in the Antebellum South*. Rev. ed. New York: Oxford University Press, 1979.

Blight, David, ed. *Passages to Freedom: The Underground Railroad in History and Memory*. New York: Smithsonian Books/HarperCollins, in association with the National Underground Railroad Freedom Center, 2004.

Blockson, Charles L. *Underground Railroad: Dramatic Firsthand Accounts of Daring Escapes to Freedom*. New York: Prentice-Hall, 1987.

Bordewich, Fergus. *Bound for Canaan: The Underground Railroad and the War for the Soul of America*. New York: Amistad Books, 2005.

Buckmaster, Henrietta. *Let My People Go: The Story of the Underground Railroad and the Growth of the Abolition Movement*. Columbia: University of South Carolina Press, 1992.

Burns, James MacGregor. *The Vineyard of Liberty*. New York: Vintage Books, 1983.

Chadwick, Bruce. *Traveling the Underground Railroad: A Visitor's Guide to More Than 300 Sites*. Secaucus, NJ: Carol Publishing Group, 1999.

Christman, Margaret C. S. *1846: Portrait of the Nation*. Washington, DC: Smithsonian Institution Press, 1996.

Davis, David Brion. *Inhuman Bondage: The Rise and Fall of Slavery in the New World*. New York: Oxford University Press, 2006.

Davis, David Brion, and Steven Mintz. *The Boisterous Sea of Liberty: A Documentary History of America from Discovery Through the Civil War*. New York: Oxford University Press, 1998.

Drewel, John Henry, and John Pemberton III. *Yoruba: Nine Centuries of African Art and Thought*. New York: Abrams, 1989.

Fields, Barbara Jeanne. *Slavery and Freedom on the Middle Ground: Maryland During the Nineteenth Century*. New Haven, CT: Yale University Press, 1985.

Fischer, David Hackett. *Liberty and Freedom: A Visual History of America's Founding Ideas*. New York: Oxford University Press, 2004.

Foner, Eric. *Forever Free: The Story of Emancipation and Reconstruction*. New York: Knopf, 2005.

———. *The Story of American Freedom*. New York: Norton, 1998.

Franklin, John Hope, and Alfred A. Moss Jr. *From Slavery to Freedom: A History of Negro Americans*. 6th ed. New York: Knopf, 1987.

Franklin, John Hope, and Loren Schweninger. *Runaway Slaves: Rebels on the Plantation*. New York: Oxford University Press, 1999.

Frost, Karolyn Smardz. *I've Got a Home in Glory Land: A Lost Tale of the Underground Railroad*. New York: Farrar, Straus and Giroux, 2007.

Gara, Larry. *The Liberty Line: The Legend of the Underground Railroad*. Lexington: University Press of Kentucky, 1961.

Griffler, Keith P. *Front Line of Freedom: African Americans and the Forging of the Underground Railroad in the Ohio Valley*. Lexington: University Press of Kentucky, 2004.

Hagedorn, Ann. *Beyond the River: The Untold Story of the Heroes of the Underground Railroad*. New York: Simon and Schuster, 2002.

Hanson, Ellen, ed. *The Underground Railroad: Life on the Road to Freedom*. Lowell, MA: Discovery Enterprises, 1993.

Haskins, Jim. *Get On Board: The Story of the Underground Railroad*. New York: Scholastic Press, 1993.

Horton, James Oliver, and Lois E. Horton. *Slavery and the Making of America*. New York: Oxford University Press, 2005.

Isaac, Rhys. *Landon Carter's Uneasy Kingdom: Revolution and Rebellion on a Virginia Plantation*. New York: Oxford University Press, 2004.

Johnson, H. U. (Homer Uri). *From Dixie to Canada: Romance and Realities of the Underground Railroad*. Vol. 1. Westport, CT: Negro Universities Press, 1970.

Kochs, Adrienne, and William Peden, eds. *The Life and Selected Writings of Thomas Jefferson*. New York: Random House, 1993.

Mazow, Leo G. *Picturing the Banjo*. University Park: Pennsylvania State University Press, 2005.

Ricks, Mary Kay. *Escape on the Pearl: The Heroic Bid for Freedom on the Underground Railroad*. New York: William Morrow, 2007.

Southgate, Joan E., and Fran Stewart. *In Their Path: A Grandmother's 519-Mile Underground Railroad Walk*. Solon, OH: Eagle Creek Press, 2004.

Stowe, Harriet Beecher. *Uncle Tom's Cabin*. Introduction by Jane Smiley. First published 1852. New York: Modern Library, 2001.

Switala, William J. *Underground Railroad in Delaware, Maryland, and West Virginia*. Mechanicsburg, PA: Stackpole Books, 2004.

Taylor, Alan. *American Colonies*. New York: Penguin, 2001.

Tobin, Jacqueline L., and Raymond G. Dobard. *Hidden in Plain View: A Secret Story of Quilts and the Underground Railroad*. New York: Doubleday, 1999.

BIOGRAPHY

Baker, Carlos. *Emerson Among the Eccentrics: A Group Portrait*. New York: Penguin, 1996.

Ball, Edward. *Slaves in the Family*. New York: Ballantine Books, 1999.

Bibb, Henry. *The Life and Adventures of Henry Bibb, an American Slave*. Introduction by Charles J. Heglar. First published 1849. Madison: University of Wisconsin Press, 2000.

Clinton, Catherine. *Harriet Tubman: The Road to Freedom*. New York: Little, Brown & Co., 2004.

Coffin, Levi. *Reminiscences of Levi Coffin, the Reputed President of the Underground Railroad*. Edited by Ben Richmond. Richmond, IN: Friends United Press, 1991.

Douglass, Frederick. *Narrative of the Life of Frederick Douglass, an American Slave*. Introduction by Kwame Anthony Appiah. First published 1845. New York: Modern Library, 2000.

Drew, Benjamin. *The Narratives of Fugitive Slaves*. First published 1856. Toronto: Prospero Books, 2000.

Edwards, Paul, ed. *The Interesting Narrative of the Life of Olaudah Equiano, or Gustavus Vassa, the African*. First published 1789. New York: Norton Critical Editions, 2000.

Hendrick, George, and Willene Hendrick, eds. *Fleeing for Freedom: Stories of the Underground Railroad as Told by Levi Coffin and William Still*. Chicago: Ivan R. Dee, 2004.

Jacobs, Harriet. *Incidents in the Life of a Slave Girl*. Introduction by Kwame Anthony Appiah. First published 1860. New York: Modern Library, 2000.

Lowry, Beverly. *Harriet Tubman: Imagining a Life*. New York: Doubleday, 2007.

McGowan, James. *Station Master on the Underground Railroad: Life and Letters of Thomas Garrett*. Moylan, PA: Whimsie Press, 1977.

Parker, John. *His Promised Land: The Autobiography of John P. Parker, Former Slave and Conductor on the Underground Railroad*. Edited by Stuart Sprague. New York: Norton, 1996.

Runyon, Randolph. *Delia Webster and the Underground Railroad*. Lexington: University Press of Kentucky, 1996.

Steward, Austin. *Twenty-Two Years a Slave and Forty Years a Freeman*. 1856. Reprint, Mineola, NY: Dover, 2004.

Thoreau, Henry David. "Civil Disobedience." In *Walden and Other Writings*, ed. Joseph Wood Krutch. First published 1854. New York: Bantam Classics, 1989.

Whitman, Walt. *The Portable Walt Whitman*. Ed. Mark Van Doren. New York: Viking, 1945, 1973.

Yetman, Norman R., ed. *Voices from Slavery: 100 Authentic Slave Narratives*. Mineola, NY: Dover, 2000.

ART

Barrett, Terry. *Interpreting Art: Reflecting, Wondering, and Responding*. New York: McGraw-Hill, 2002.

Bearden, Romare, and Harry Henderson. *A History of African-American Artists: From 1792 to the Present*. New York: Pantheon Books, 1993.

Birren, Faber. *Color and Human Response: Aspects of Light and Color Bearing on the Reactions of Living Things and the Welfare of Human Beings*. New York: Wiley, 2005.

——— ed. *A Grammar of Color: A Basic Treatise on the Color System of Albert H. Munsell*. First published 1926. New York: Van Nostrand Reinhold Co., 1969.

Chevreul, Michel-Eugène. *The Principles of Harmony and Contrast of Colors*. Edited by Faber Birren. First published 1839. New York: Reinhold, 1967.

Da Vinci, Leonardo. *A Treatise on Painting*. 1877. Reprint, Mineola, NY: Dover, 2005.

Düchting, Hajo. *Paul Klee: Painting and Music*. New York: Prestel, 2004.

Fine, Ruth, et al. *The Art of Romare Bearden*. Washington, DC: National Gallery of Art, 2003.

Gage, John. *Color and Meaning: Art, Science, and Symbolism*. Berkeley: University of California Press, 1999.

Graham, John D. *System and Dialectics of Art*. New York: Delphic Studios, 1937.

Haward, Lawrence. *Music in Painting*. New York: Pitman, 1948.

Kandinsky, Wassily. *Concerning the Spiritual in Art*. 1914. Reprint, Mineola, NY: Dover, 1977. Originally published as *The Art of Spiritual Harmony*.

Nesbett, Peter. *Over the Line: The Art and Life of Jacob Lawrence*. Washington, DC: Phillips Collection, 2001.

Wellington, Hubert. *The Journal of Eugène Delacroix*. Ithaca, NY: Cornell University Press, 1980.

Wilmerding, John. *American Light: The Luminist Movement, 1850–1875*. Princeton, NJ: Princeton University Press, 1989.

COLOR IN FREEDOM: PLATES

THE FIRST MOVEMENT: The Unknown World

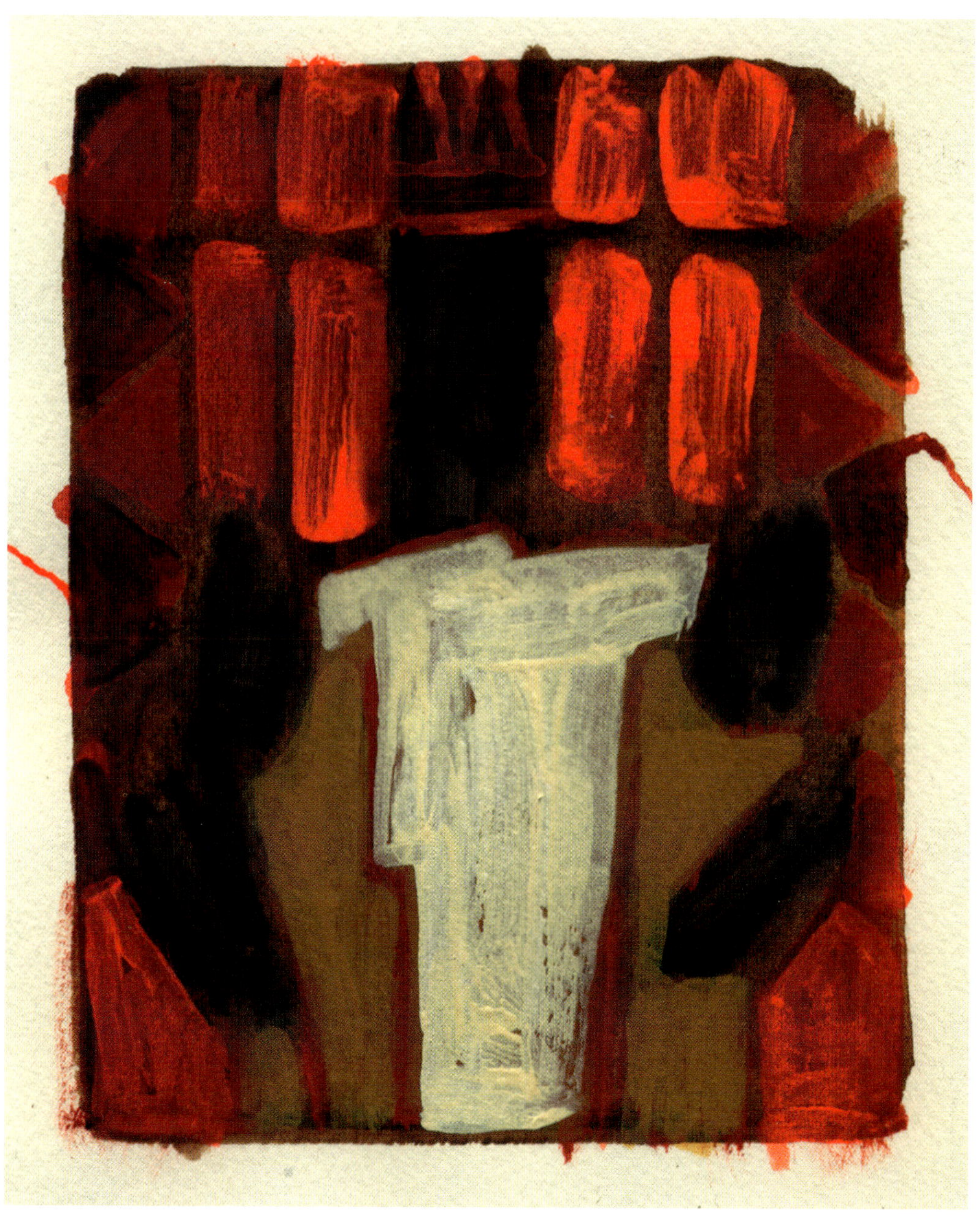

Protection (Study), 2008. Acrylic on paper, 5¾ x 4½ in.

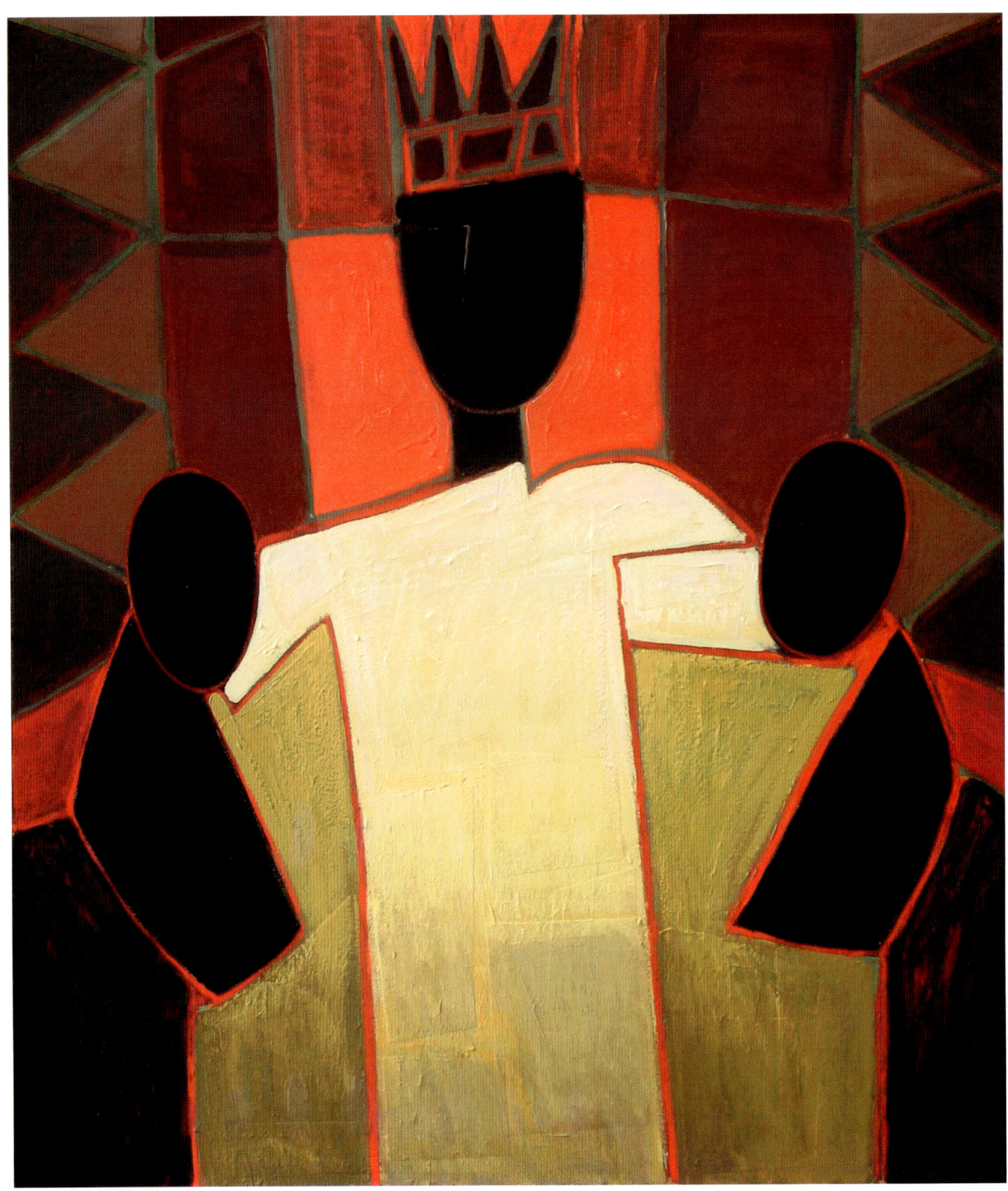

Protection, 2008. Mixed media, 48 x 42 in.

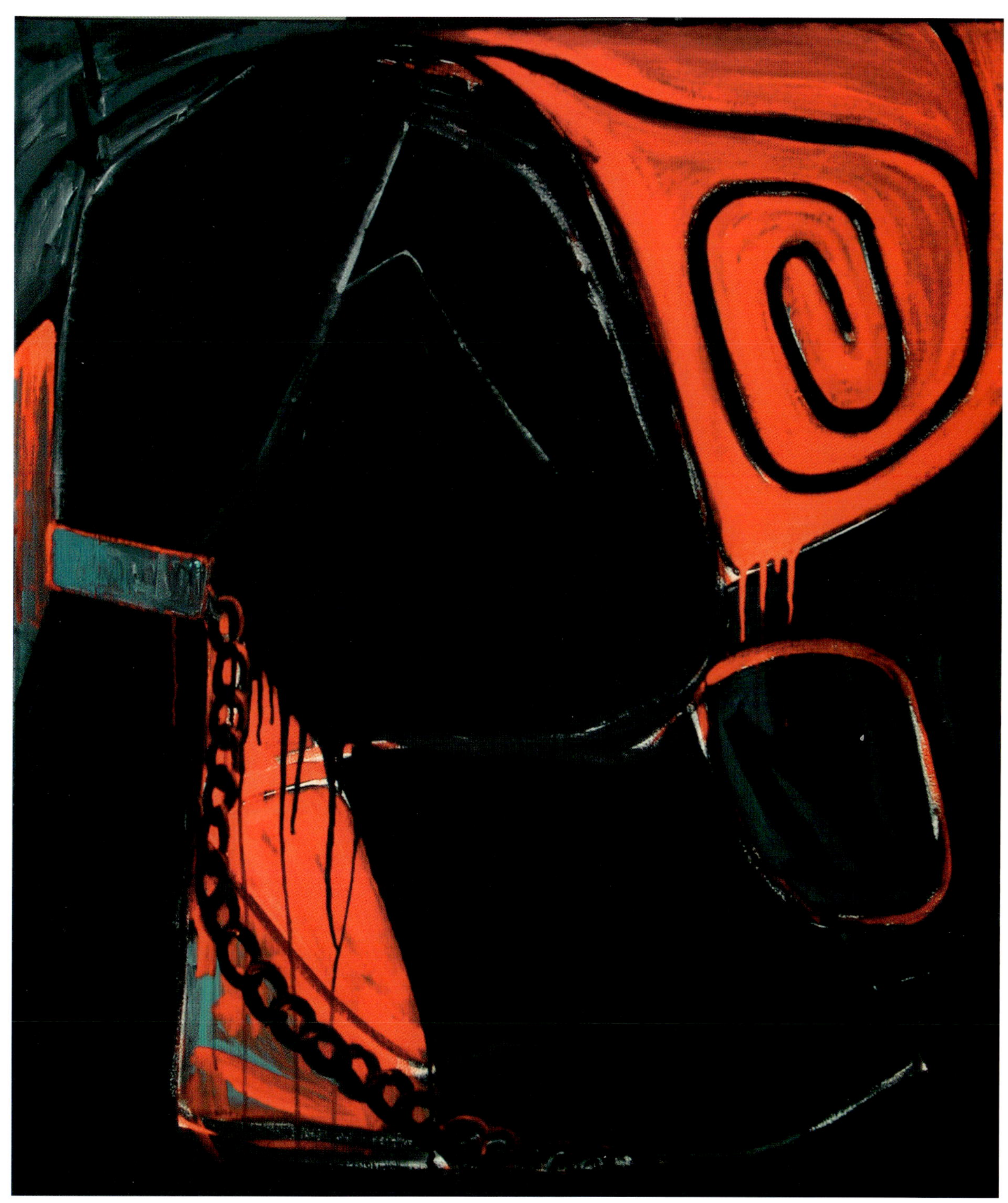

Contemplation of Despair, 2008. Mixed media, 48 x 42 in.

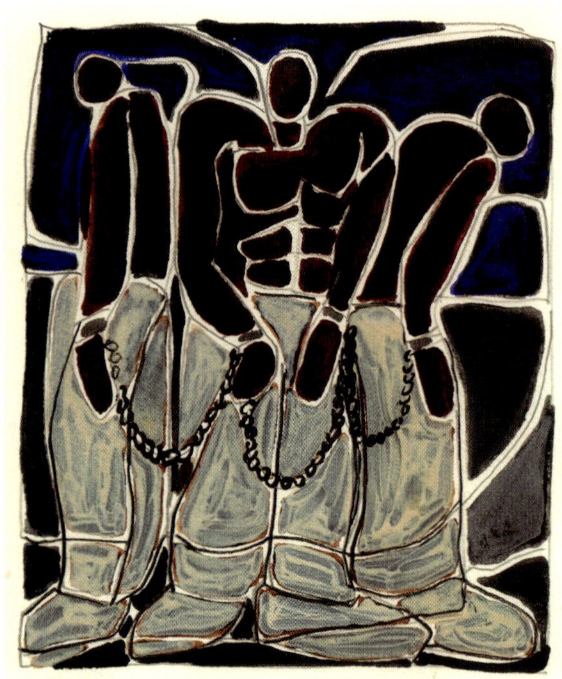

Subjugation (Study), 2008. Acrylic on paper, 7¾ x 6½ in.

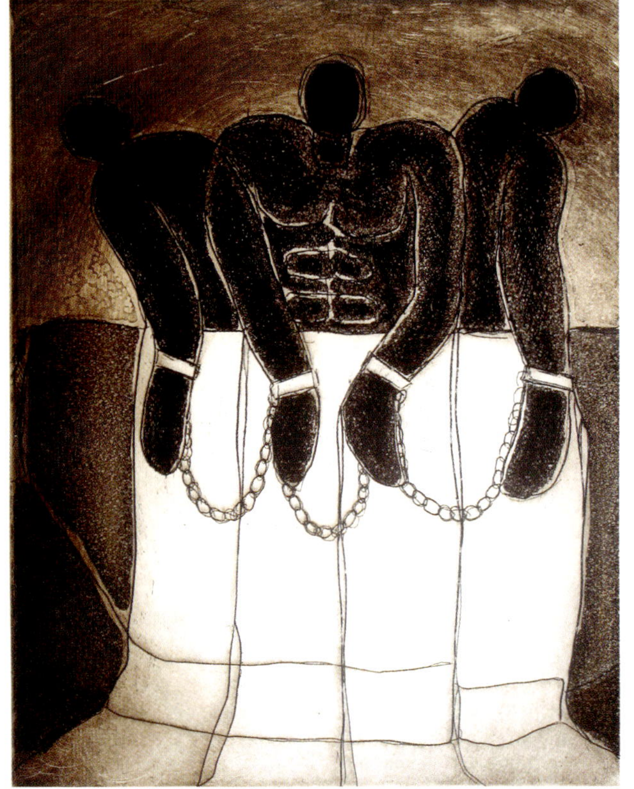

Subjugation, 2008. Etching, 14 x 11 in.

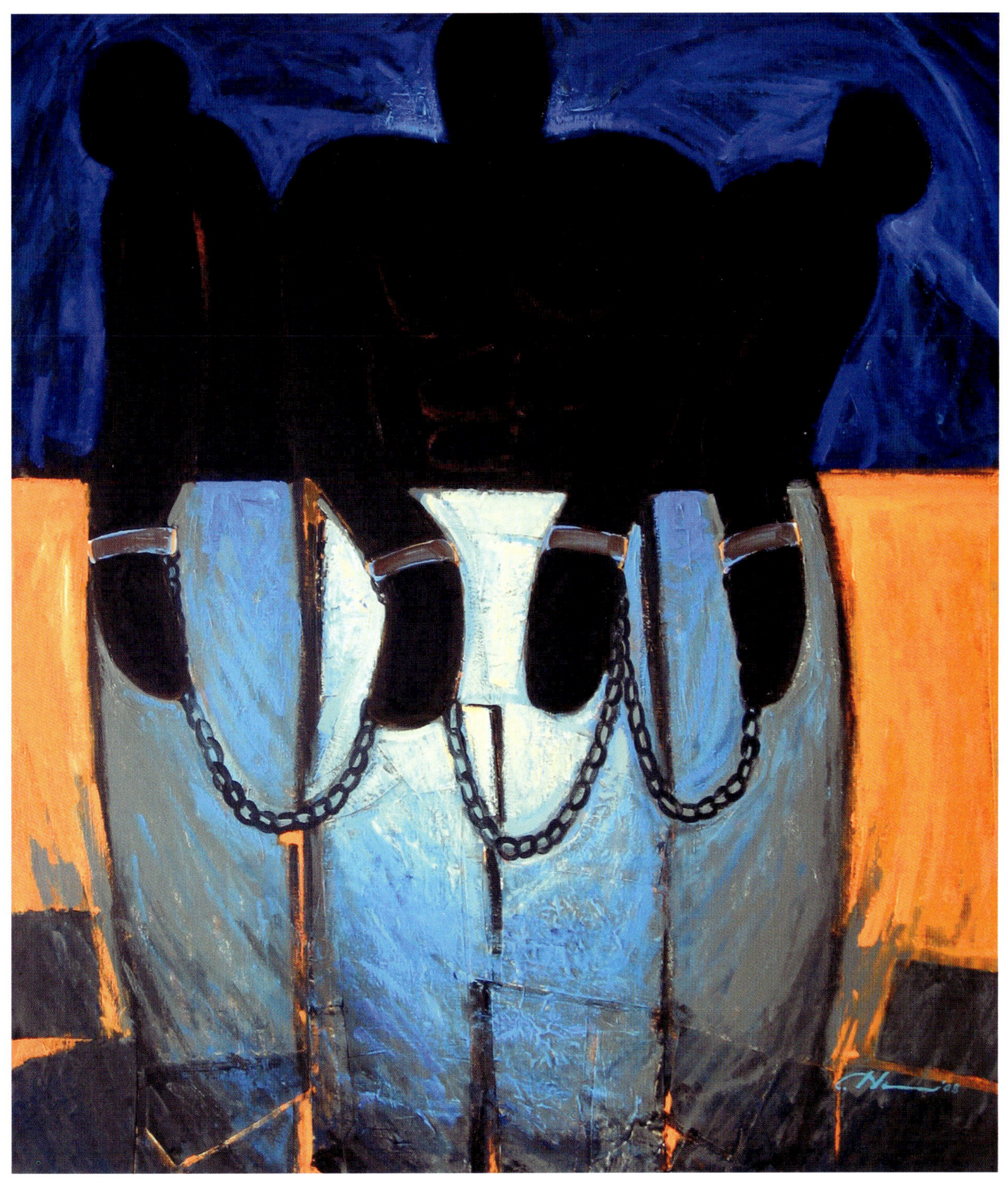

Subjugation, 2008. Mixed media, 48 x 42 in.

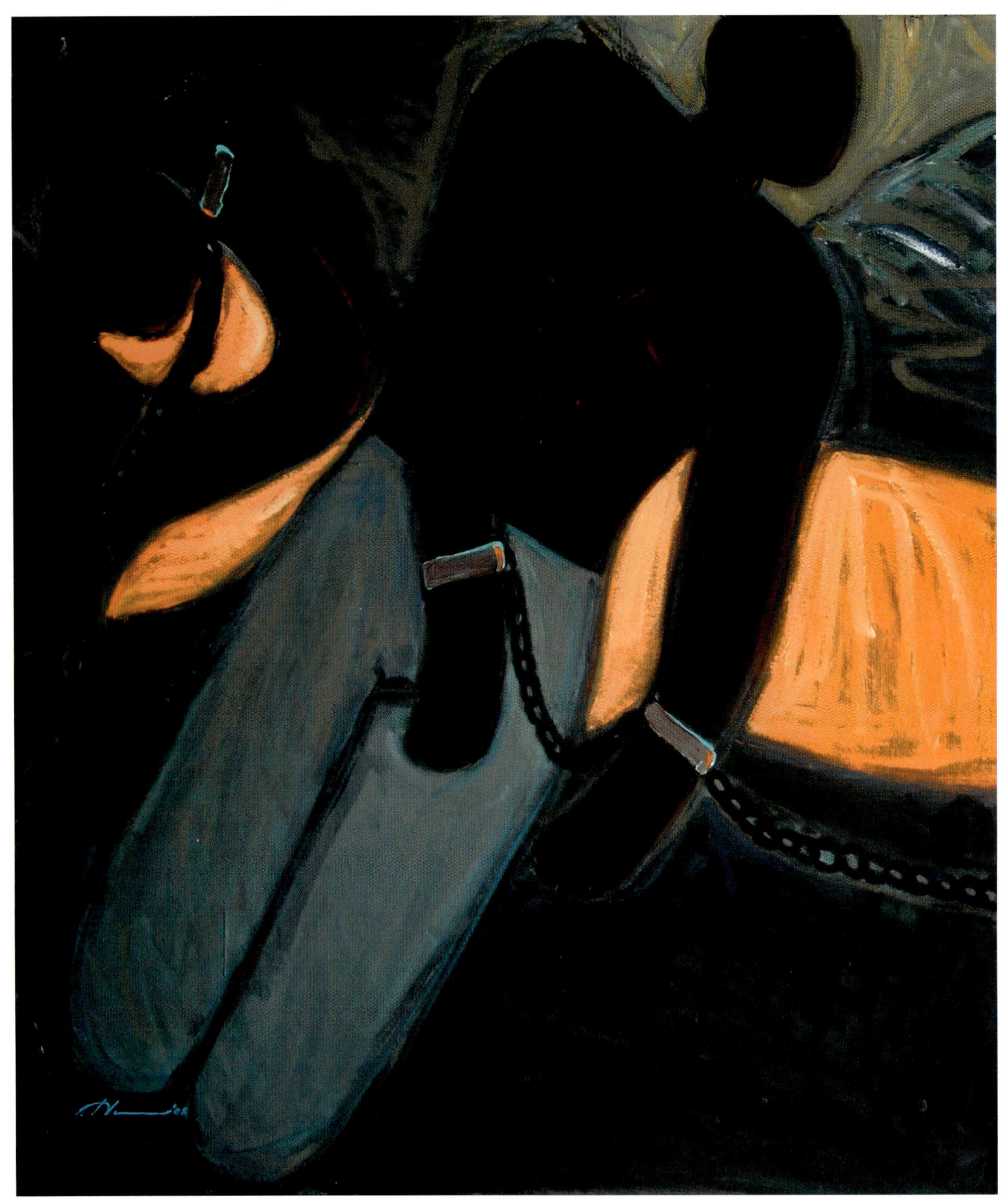

Middle Passage, 2008. Acrylic on canvas, 48 x 42 in.

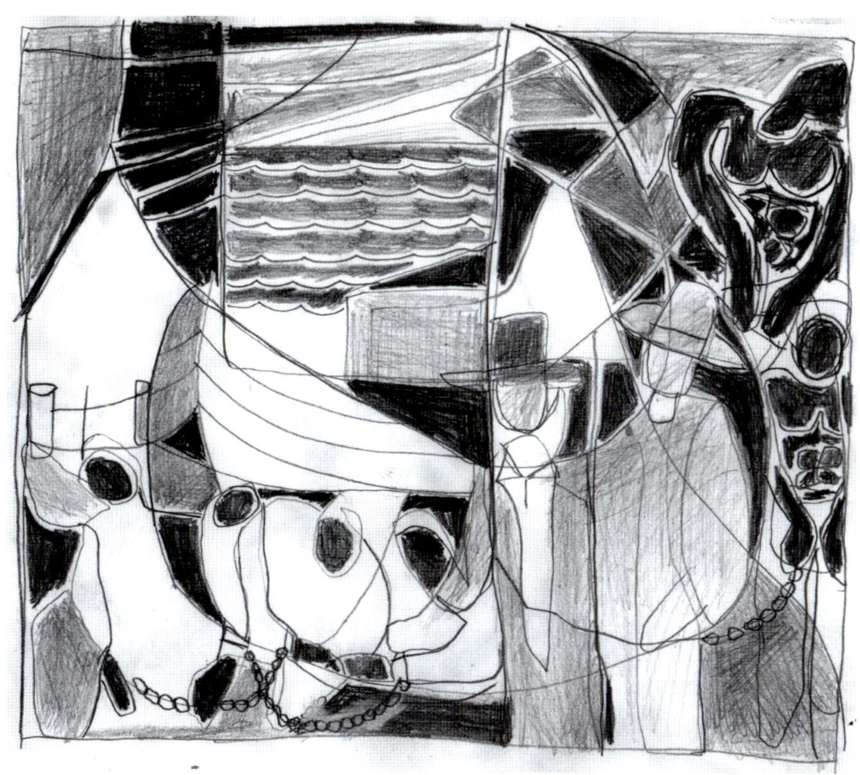

Arrival in the Unknown (Study),
2008. Pencil, 7¾ x 9¼ in.

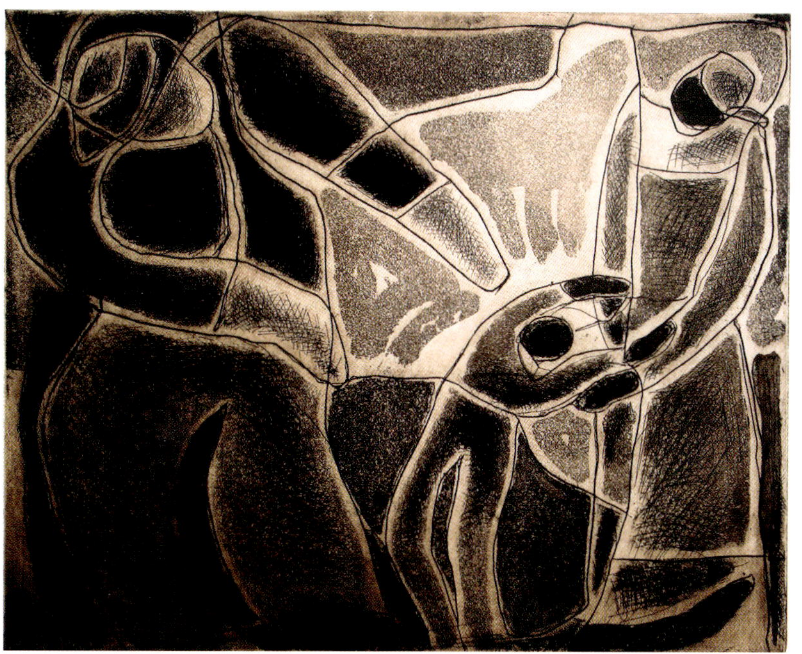

Unbearable Loss, 2008.
Etching, 11 x 14 in.

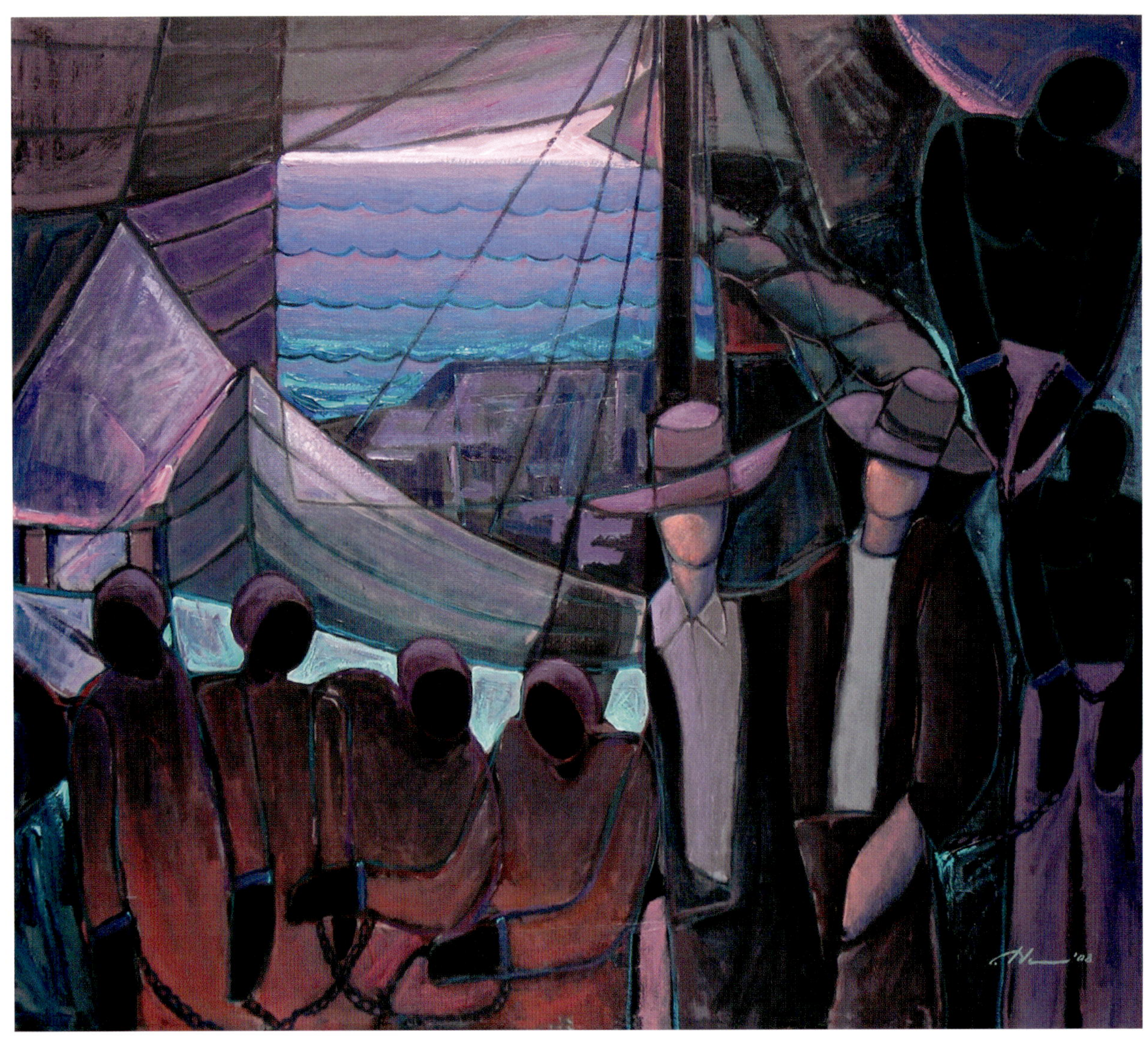

Arrival in the Unknown, 2008. Mixed media, 42 x 48 in.

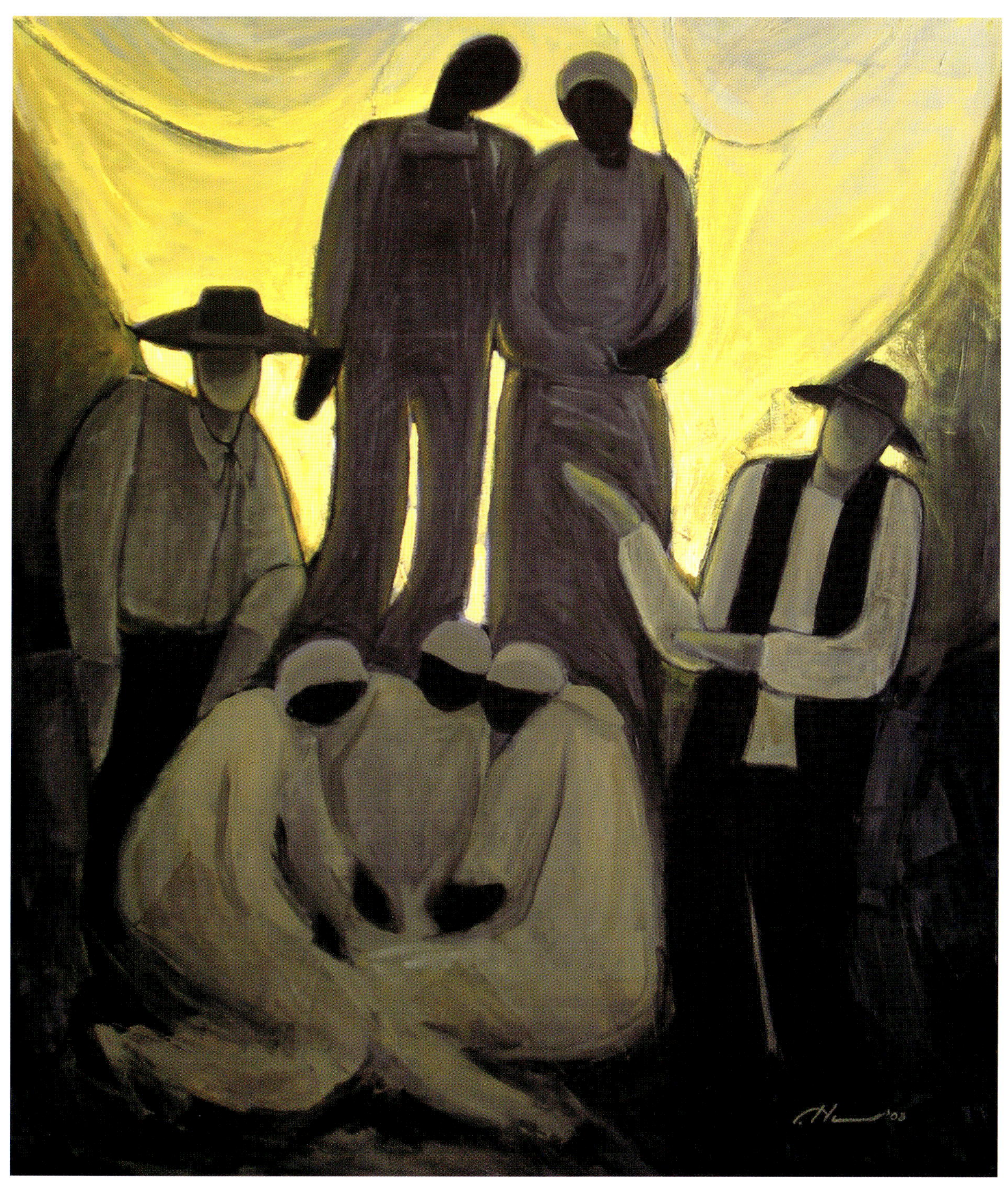

On the Block, 2008. Mixed media, 48 x 42 in.

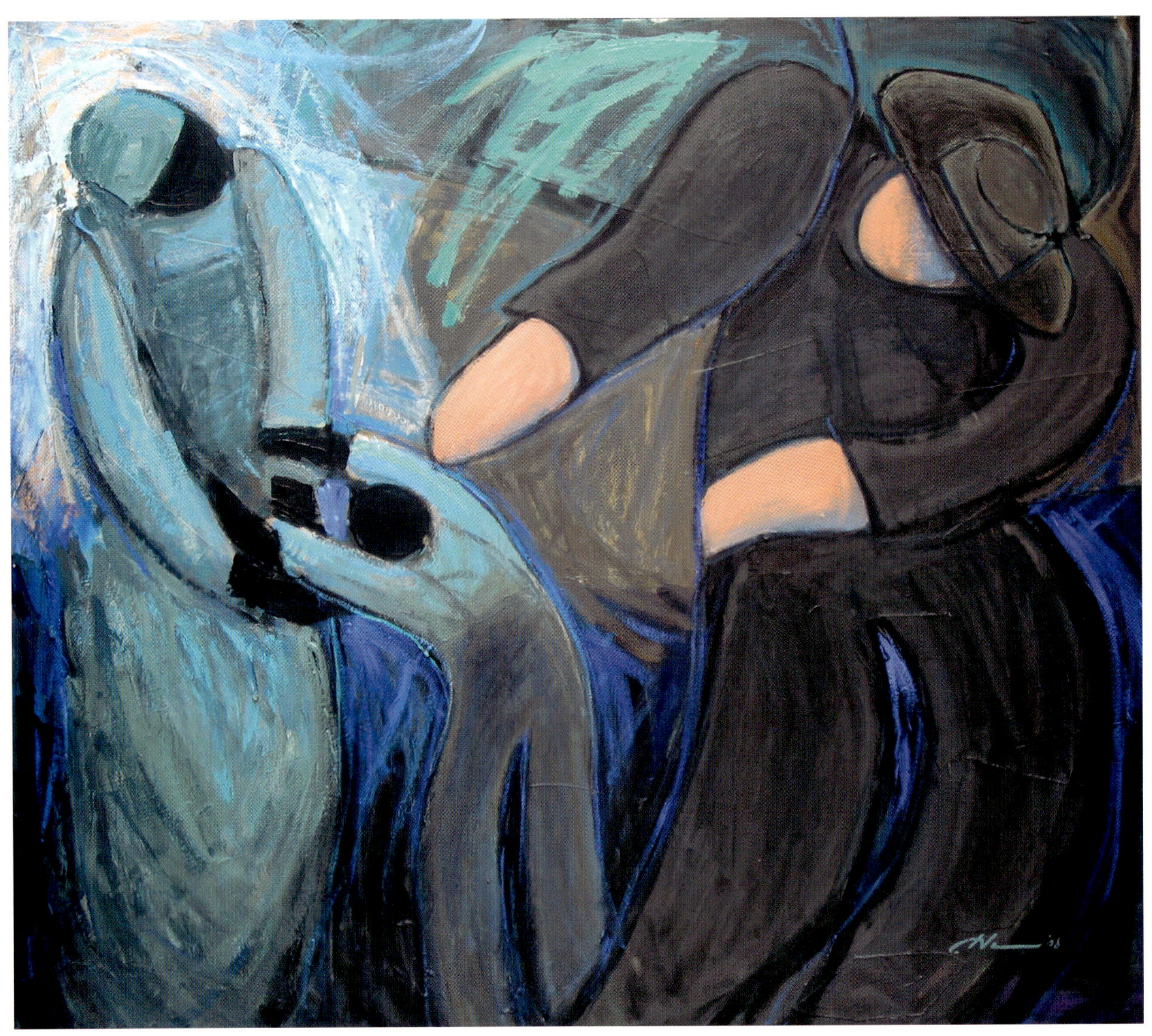

Unbearable Loss, 2008. Mixed media, 42 x 48 in.

THE SECOND MOVEMENT:

Living in Bondage—Life on the Plantation

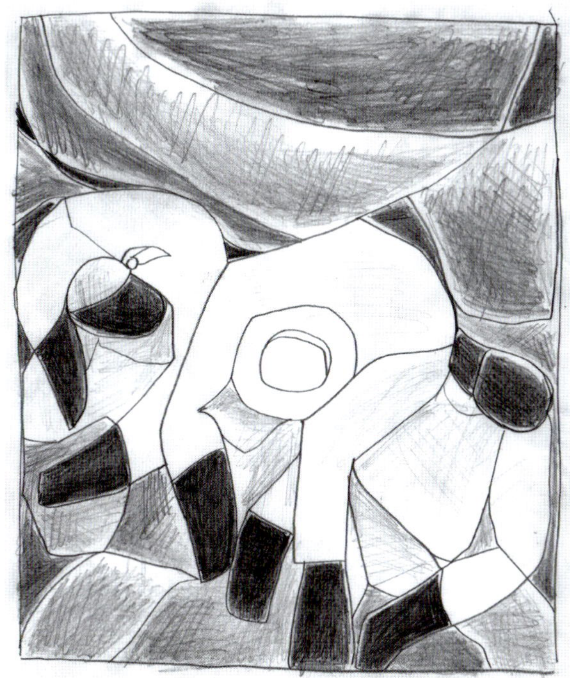

Dawn of Despair (Study), 2008. Pencil, 9¼ x 8 in.

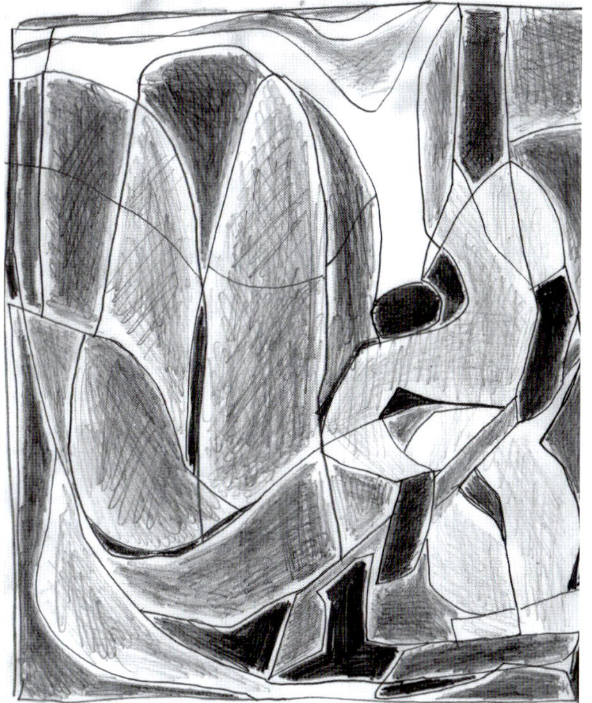

Private Plot (Study), 2008. Pencil, 9 x 8 in.

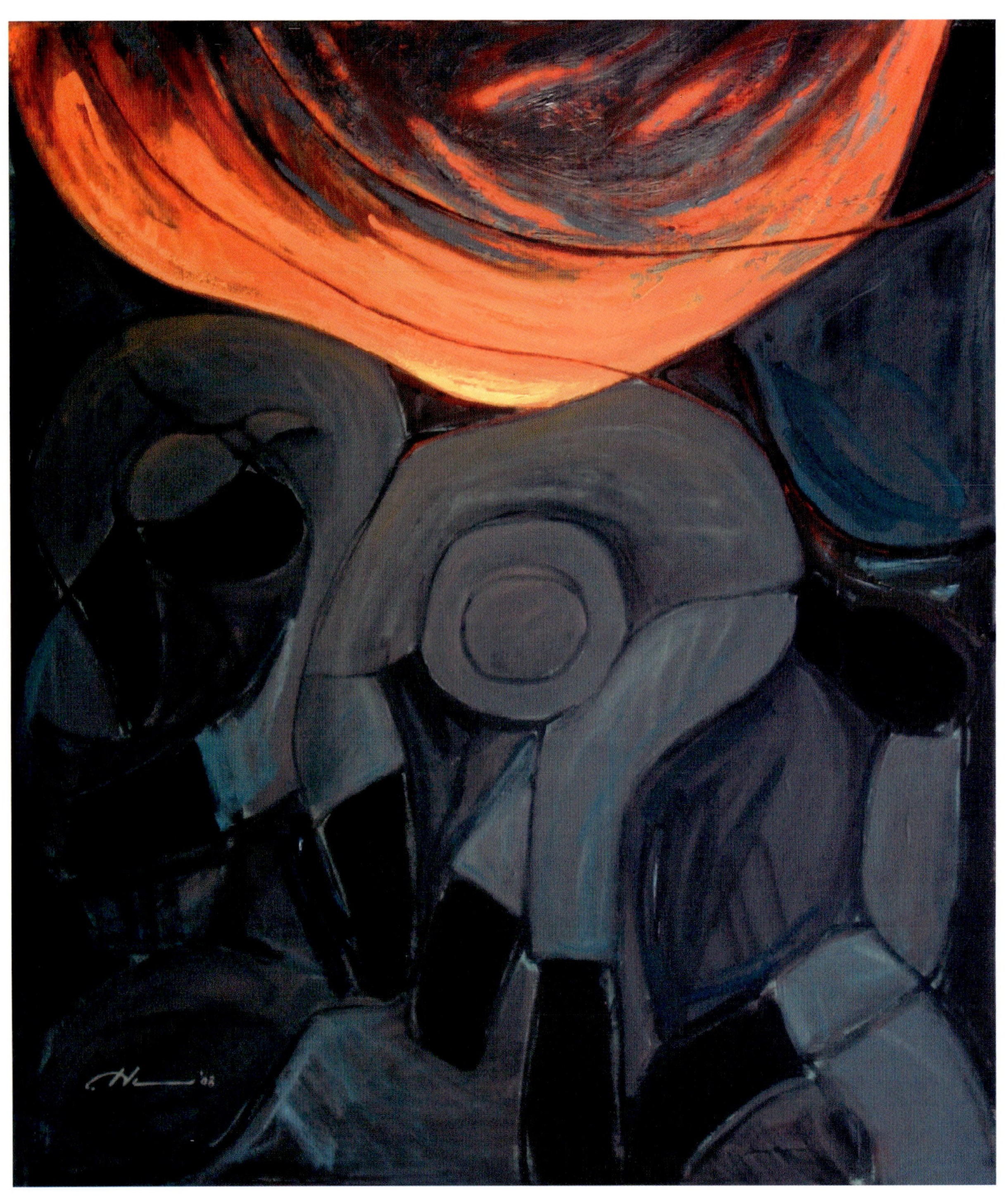

Dawn of Despair, 2008. Acrylic on canvas, 48 x 42 in.

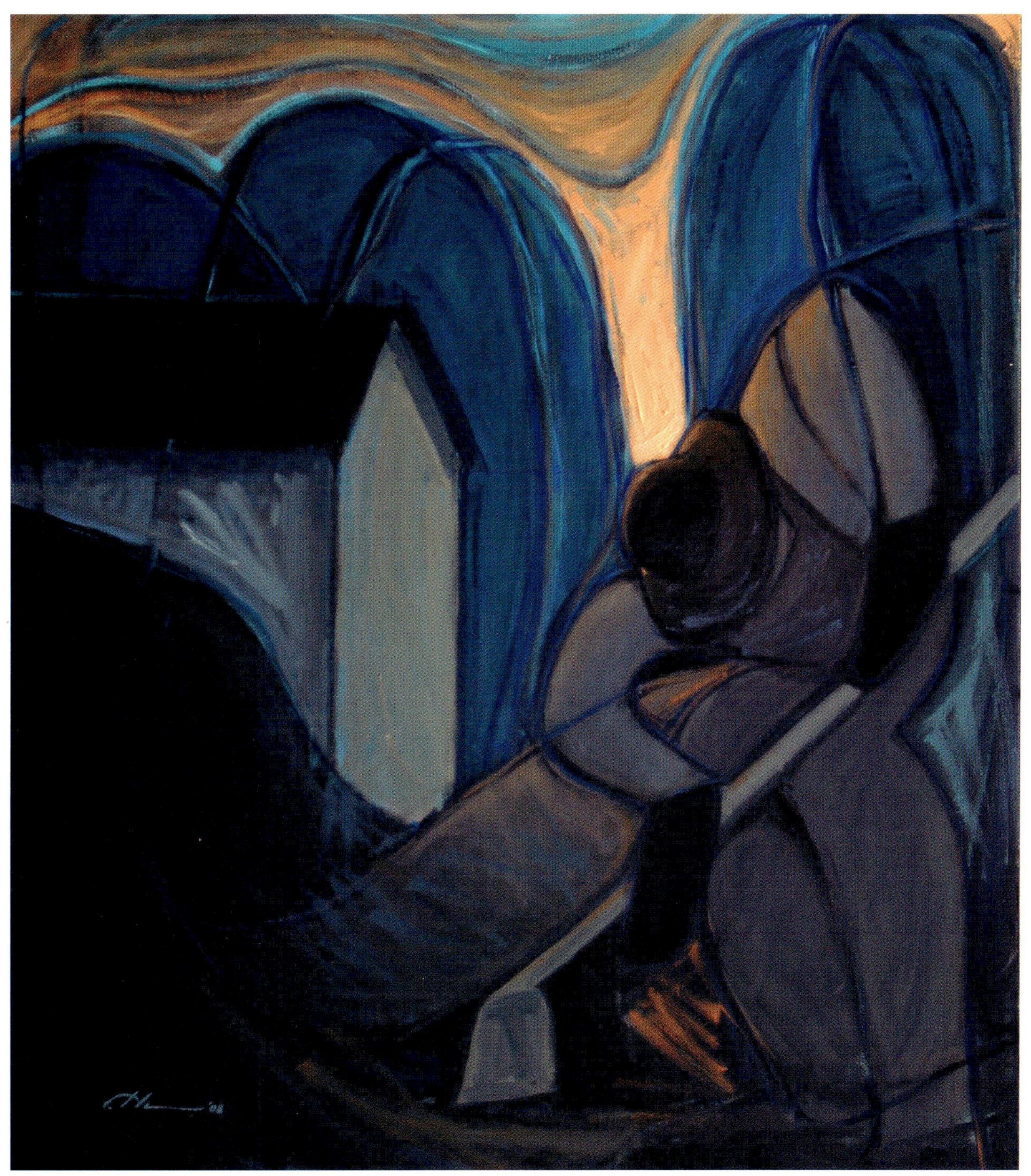

Private Plot, 2008. Acrylic on canvas, 48 x 42 in.

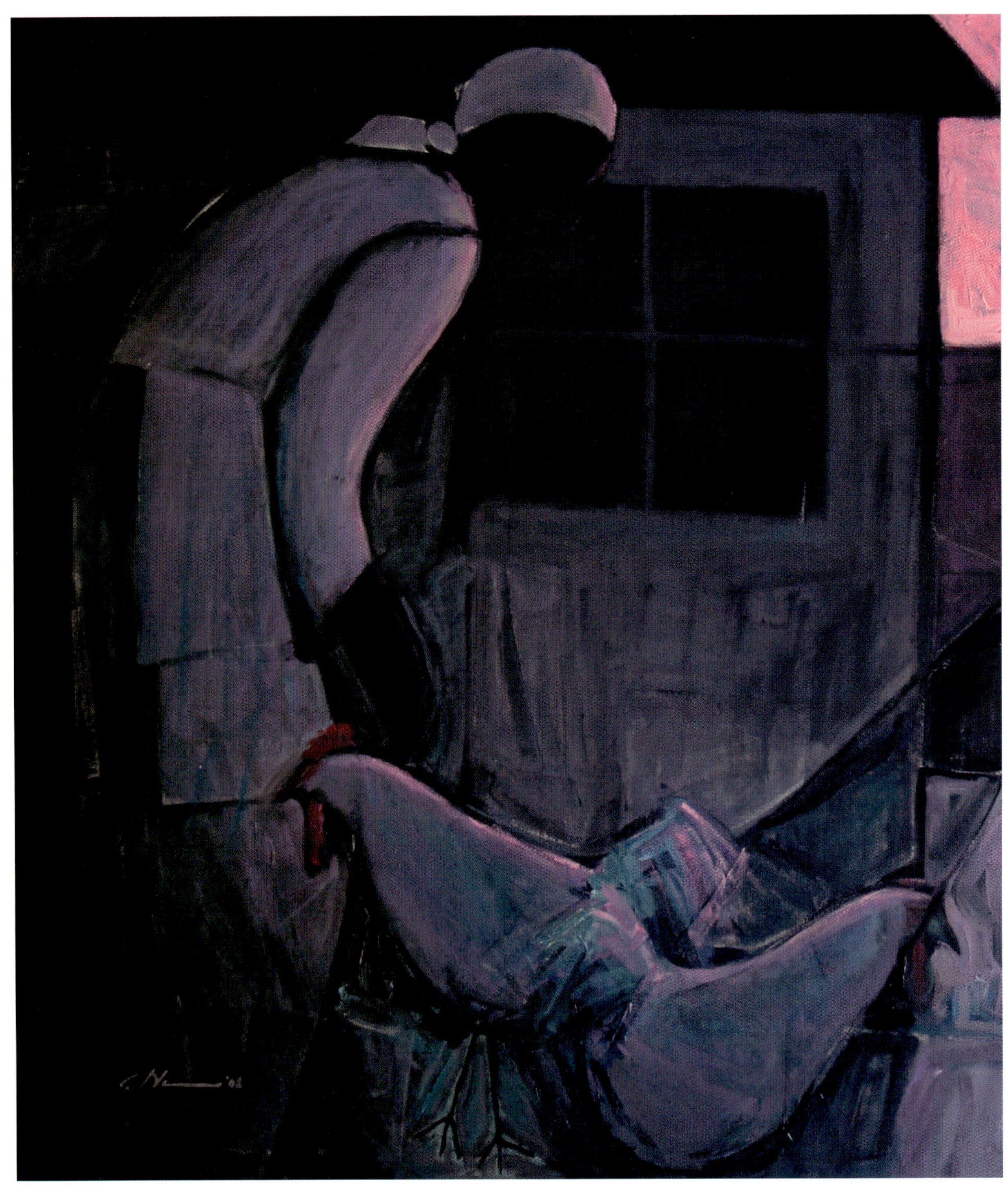

Place of Respite, 2008. Mixed media, 48 x 42 in.

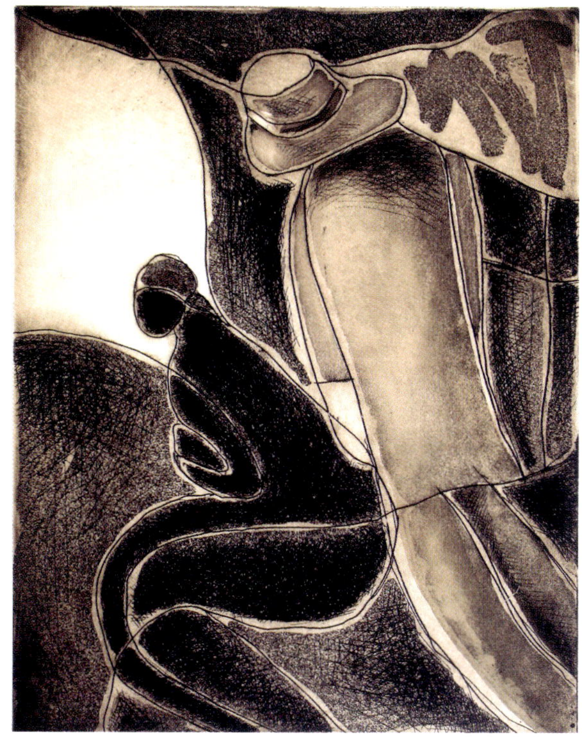

Rape, 2008. Etching, 14 x 11 in.

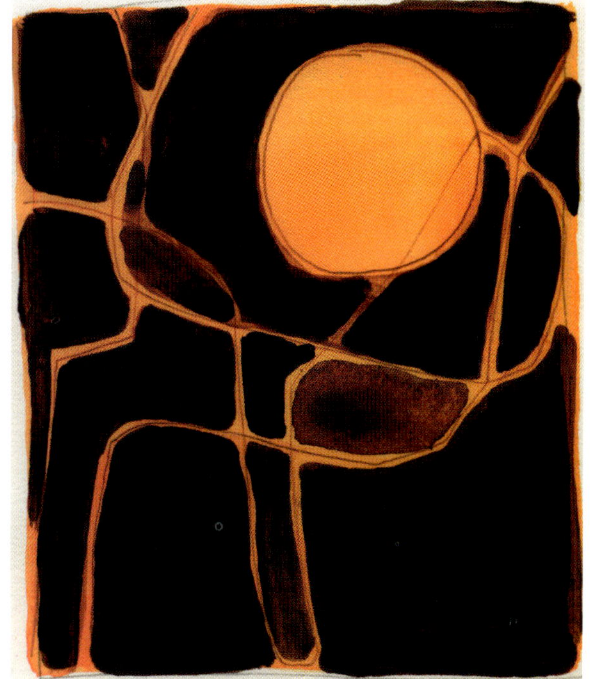

The Quarters (Study), 2008. Acrylic on paper, 6½ x 5½ in.

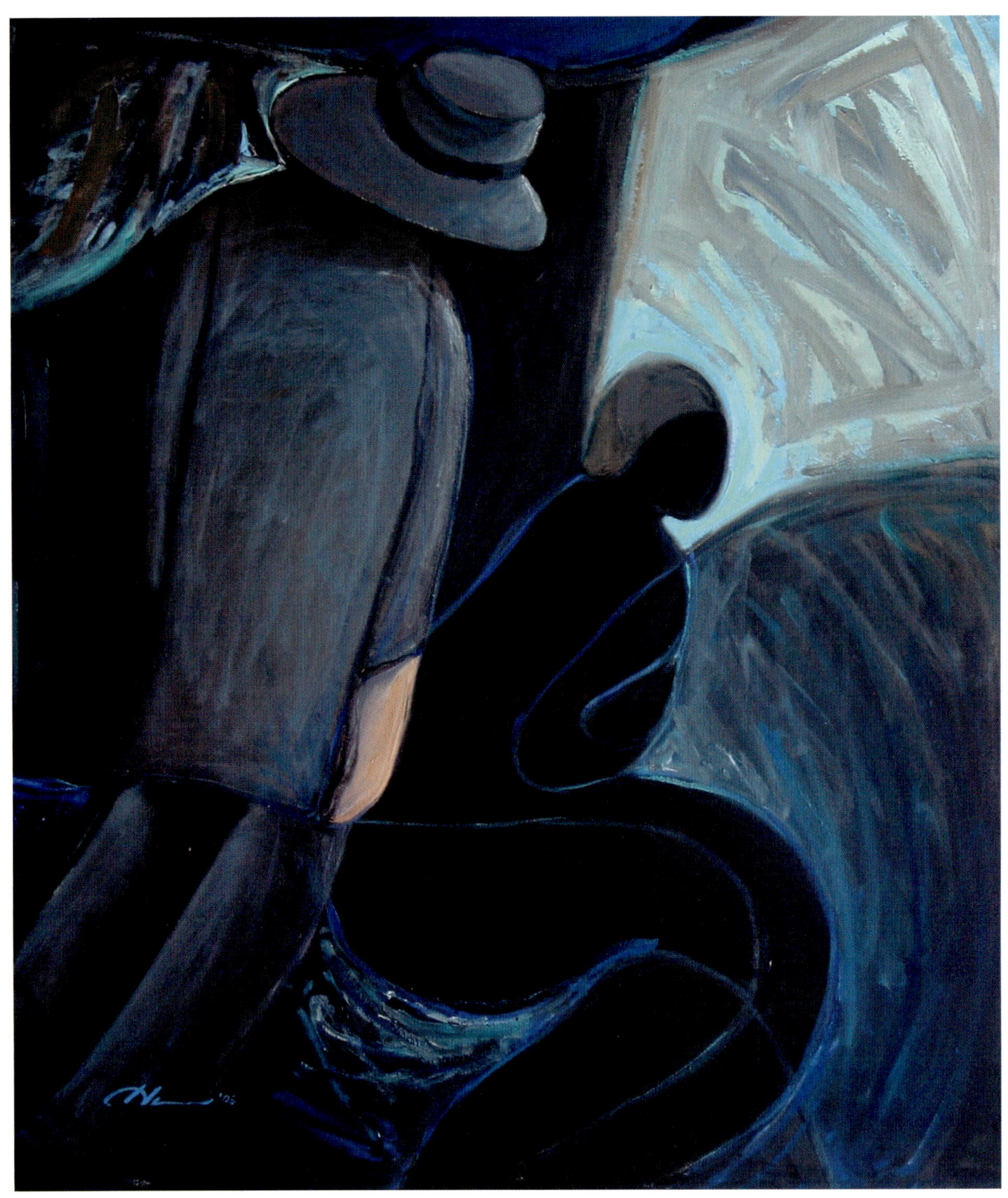

Rape, 2008. Acrylic on canvas, 48 x 42 in.

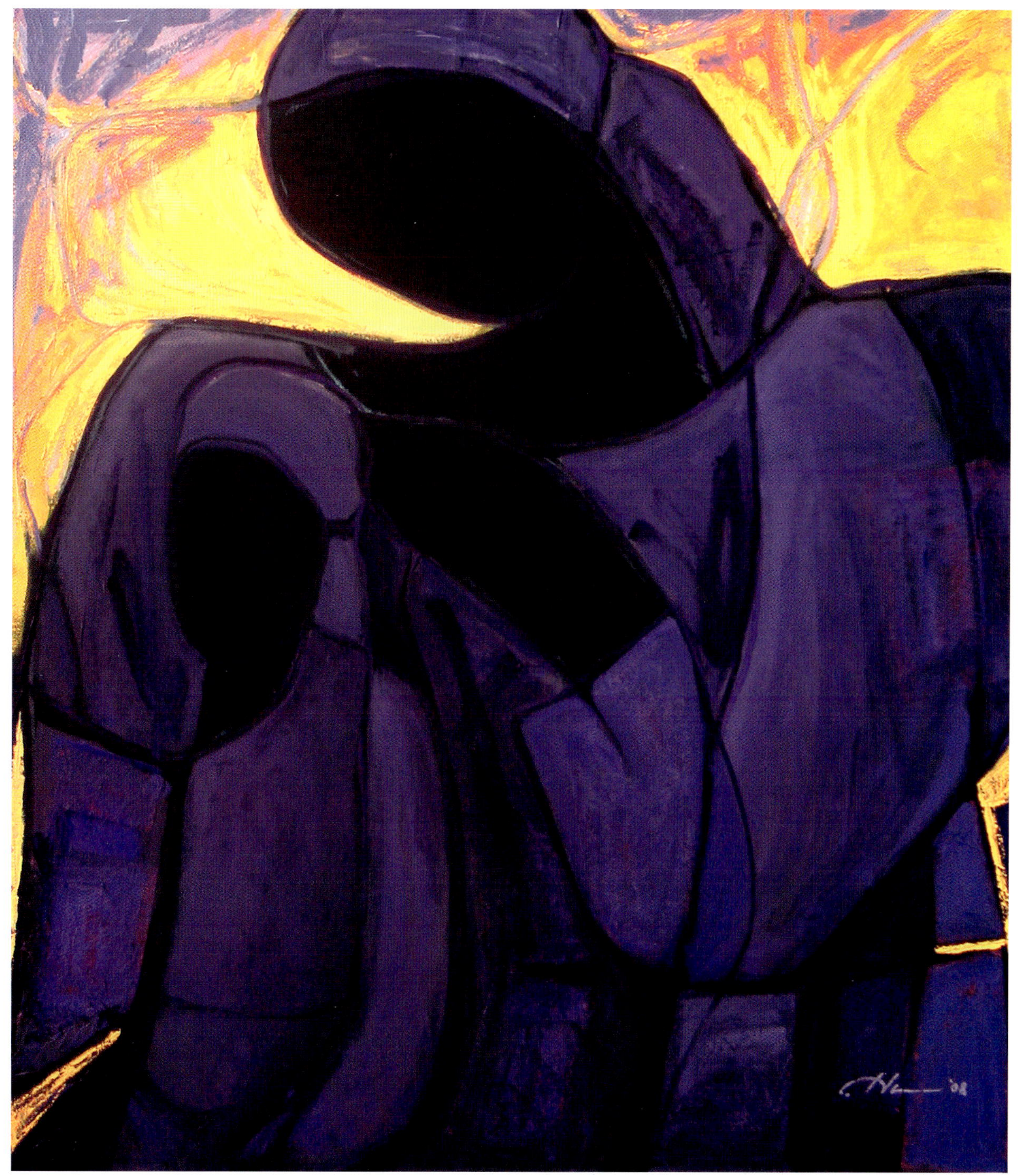

Madonna and Child, 2008. Mixed media, 48 x 42 in.

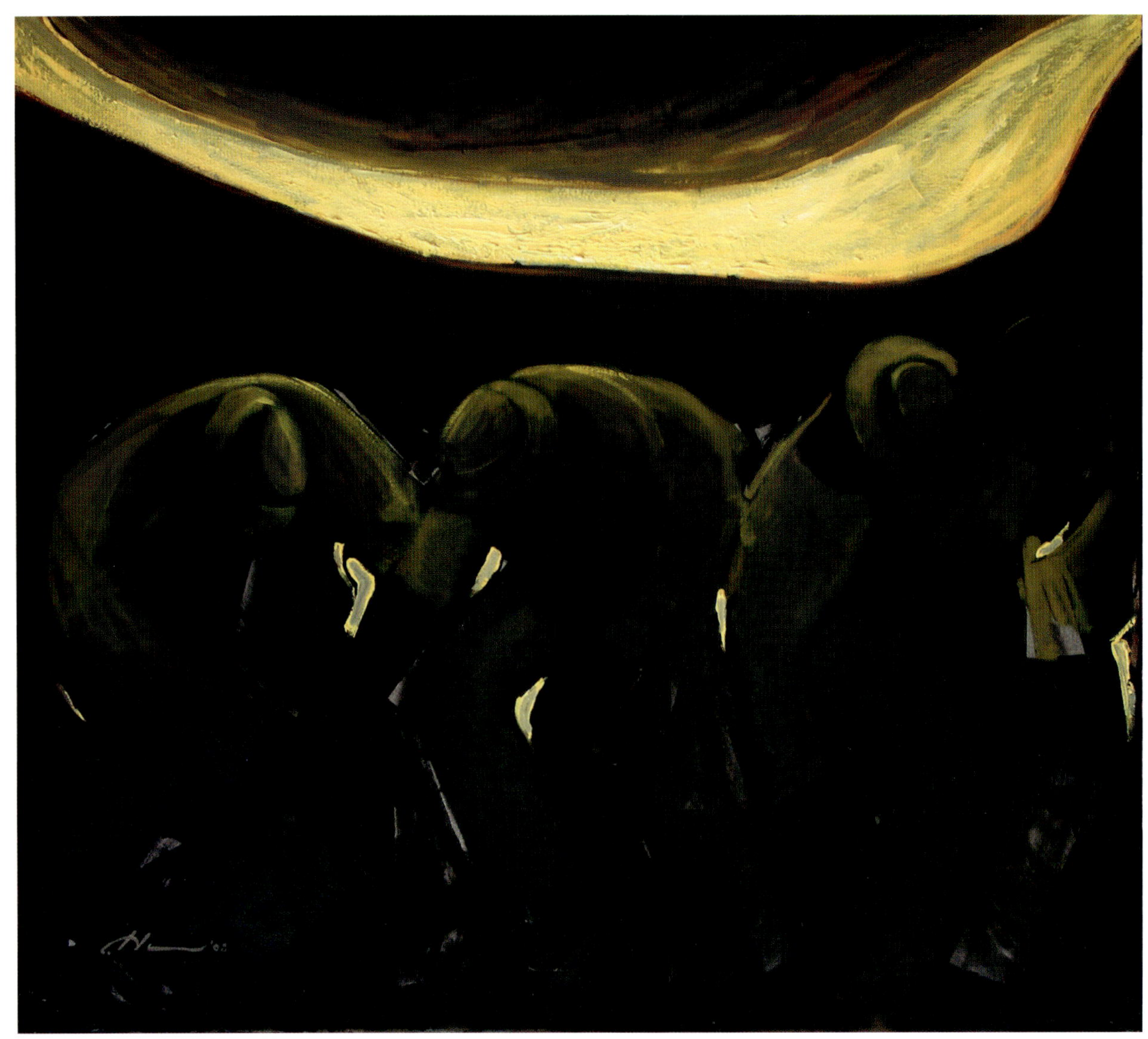

Betimes, 2008. Mixed media, 42 x 48 in.

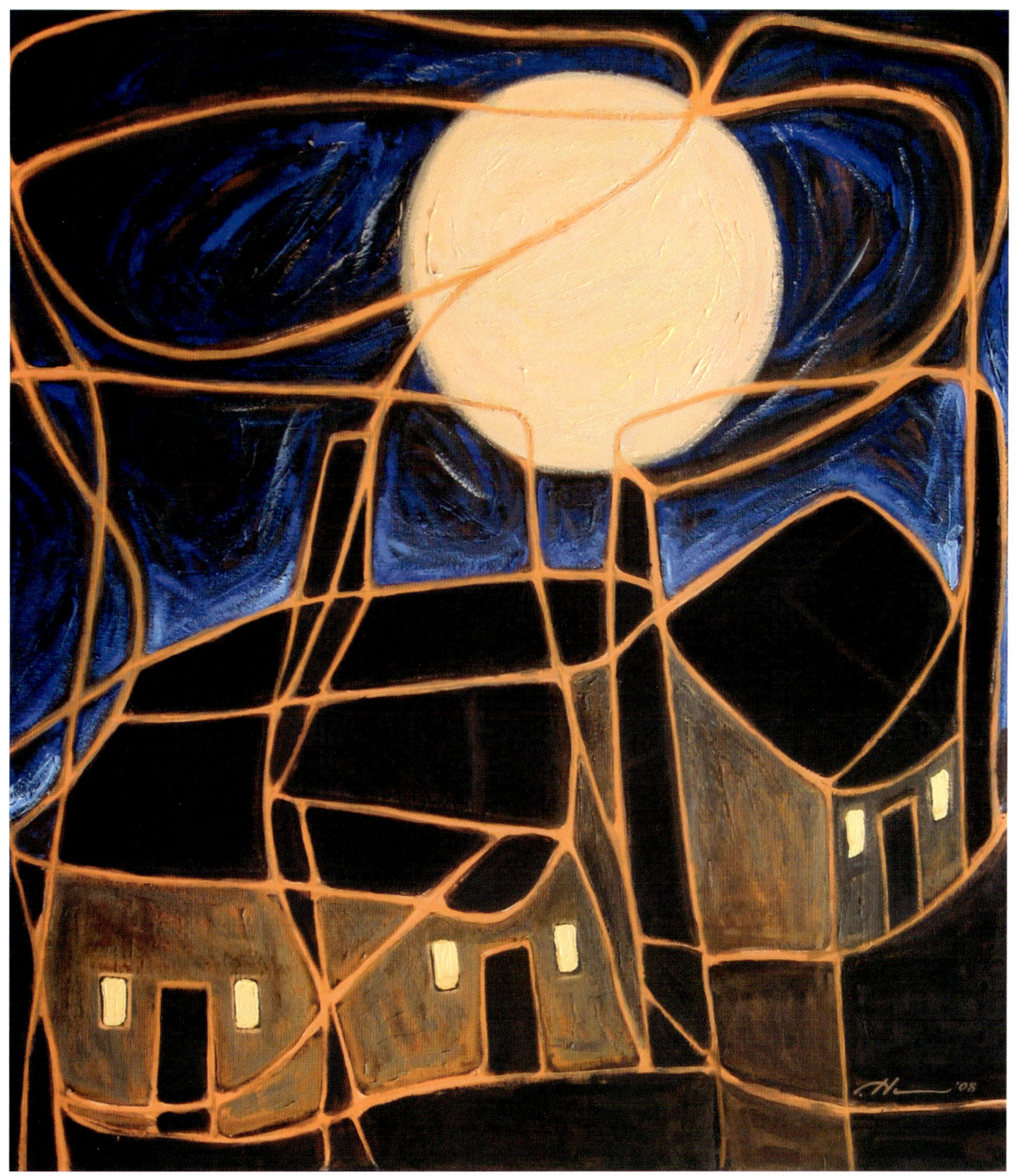

The Quarters, 2008. Mixed media, 48 x 42 in.

THE THIRD MOVEMENT: Journey of Escape

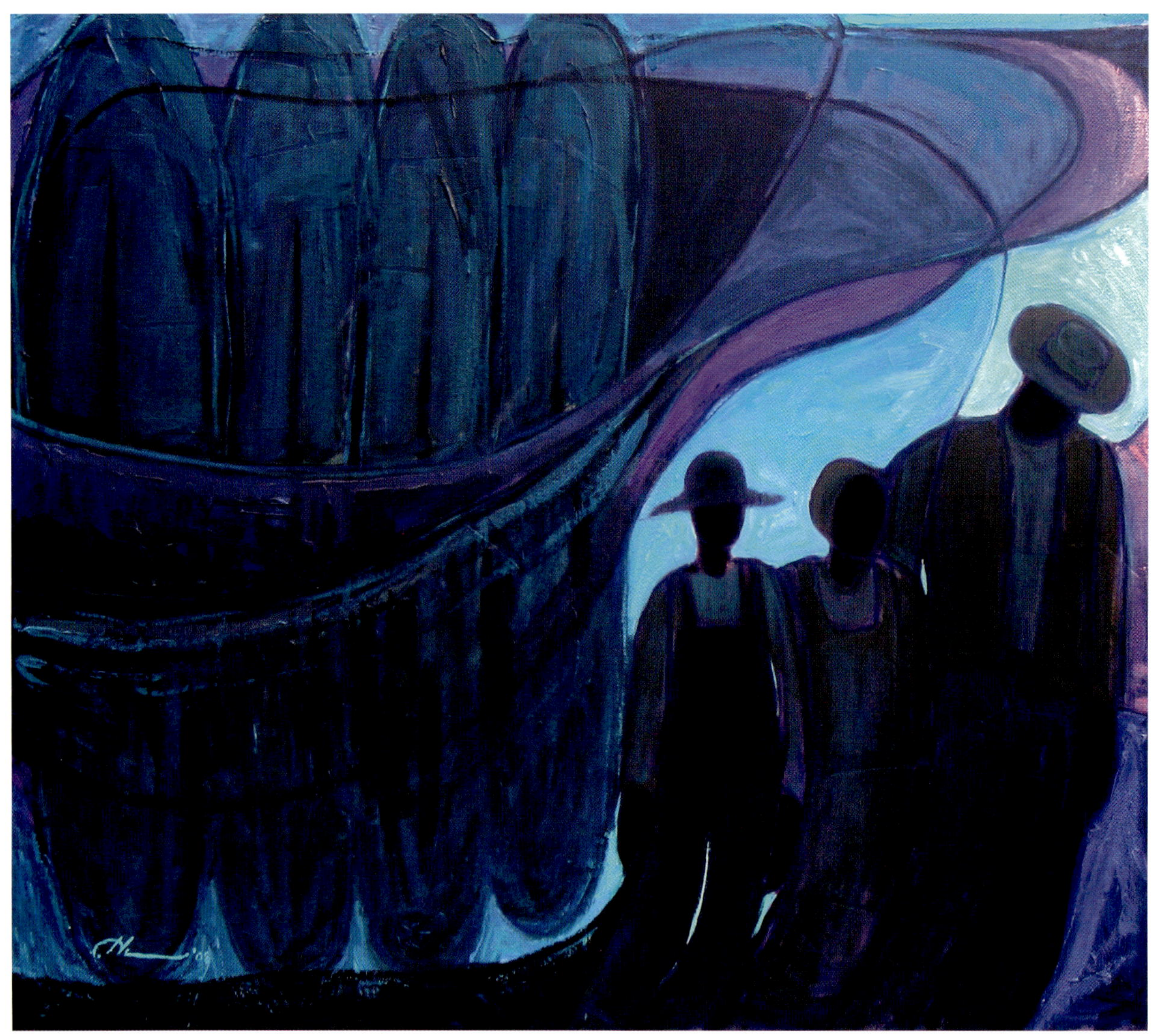

The Long Road, 2008. Mixed media, 42 x 48 in.

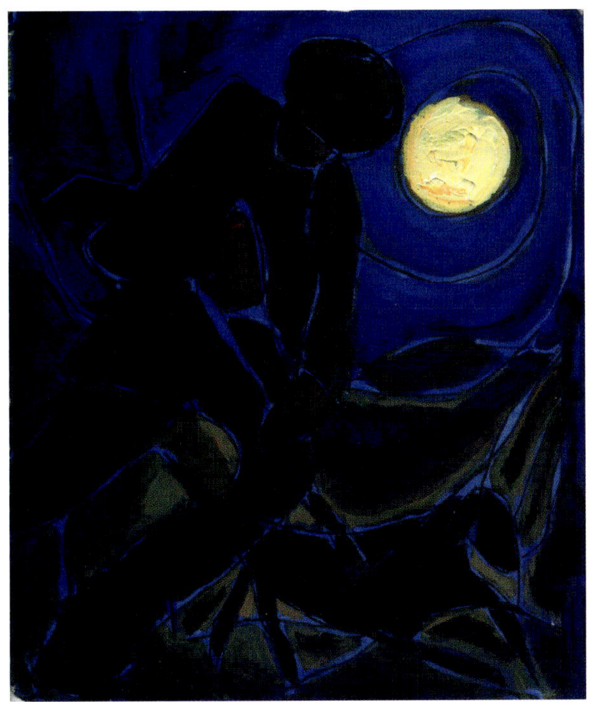

Patter-Roller (Study), 2008. Acrylic on paper, 8½ x 7¼ in.

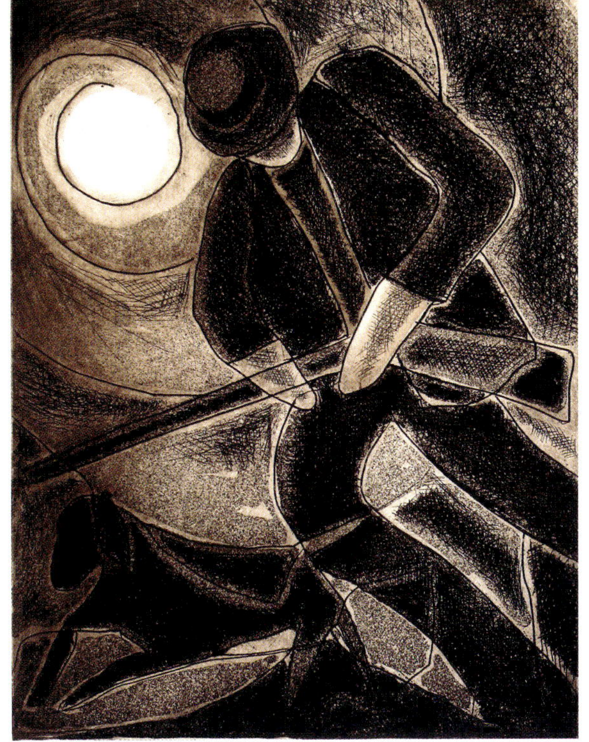

Patter-Roller, 2008. Etching, 14 x 11 in.

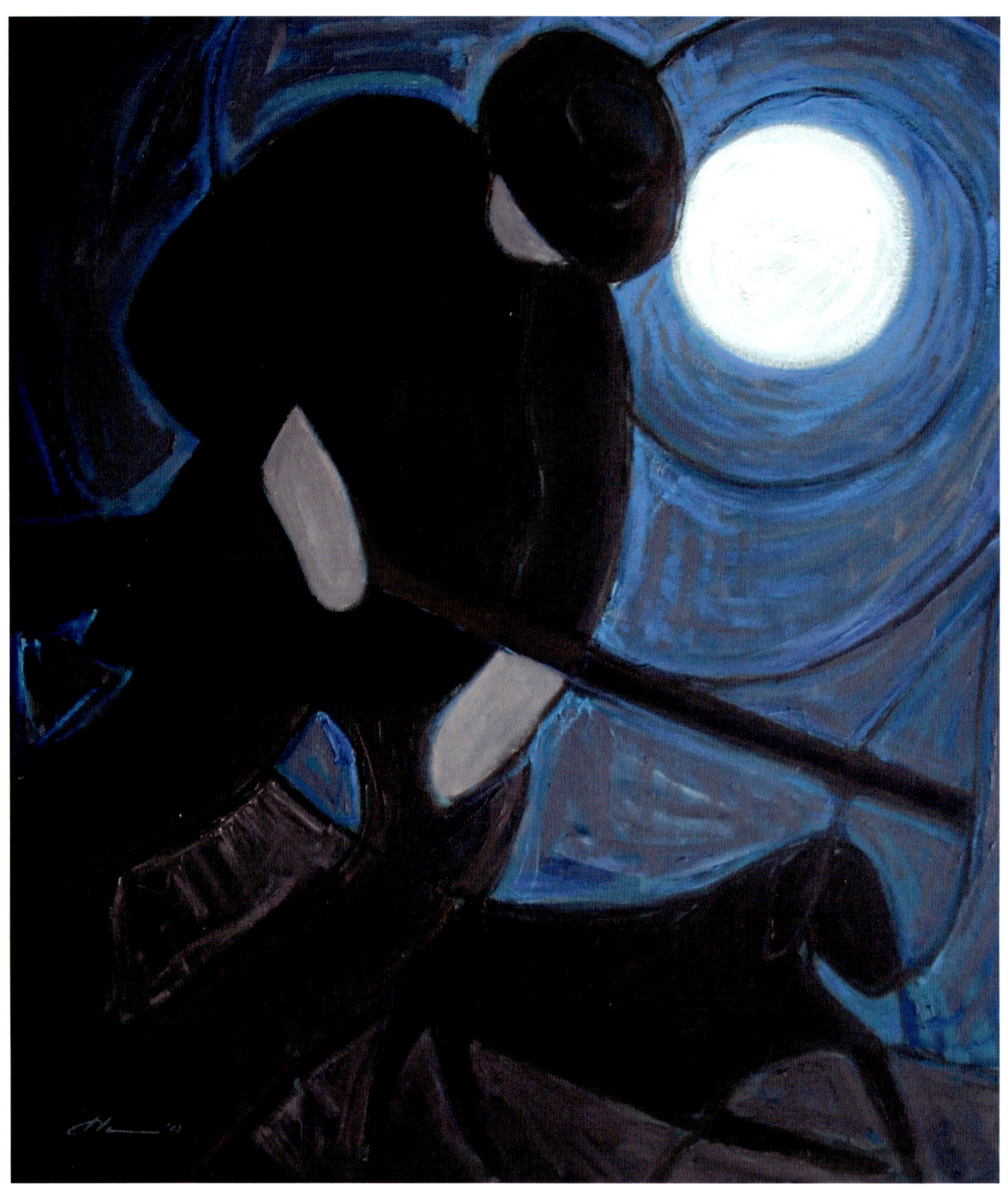

Patter-Roller, 2008. Acrylic on canvas, 48 x 42 in.

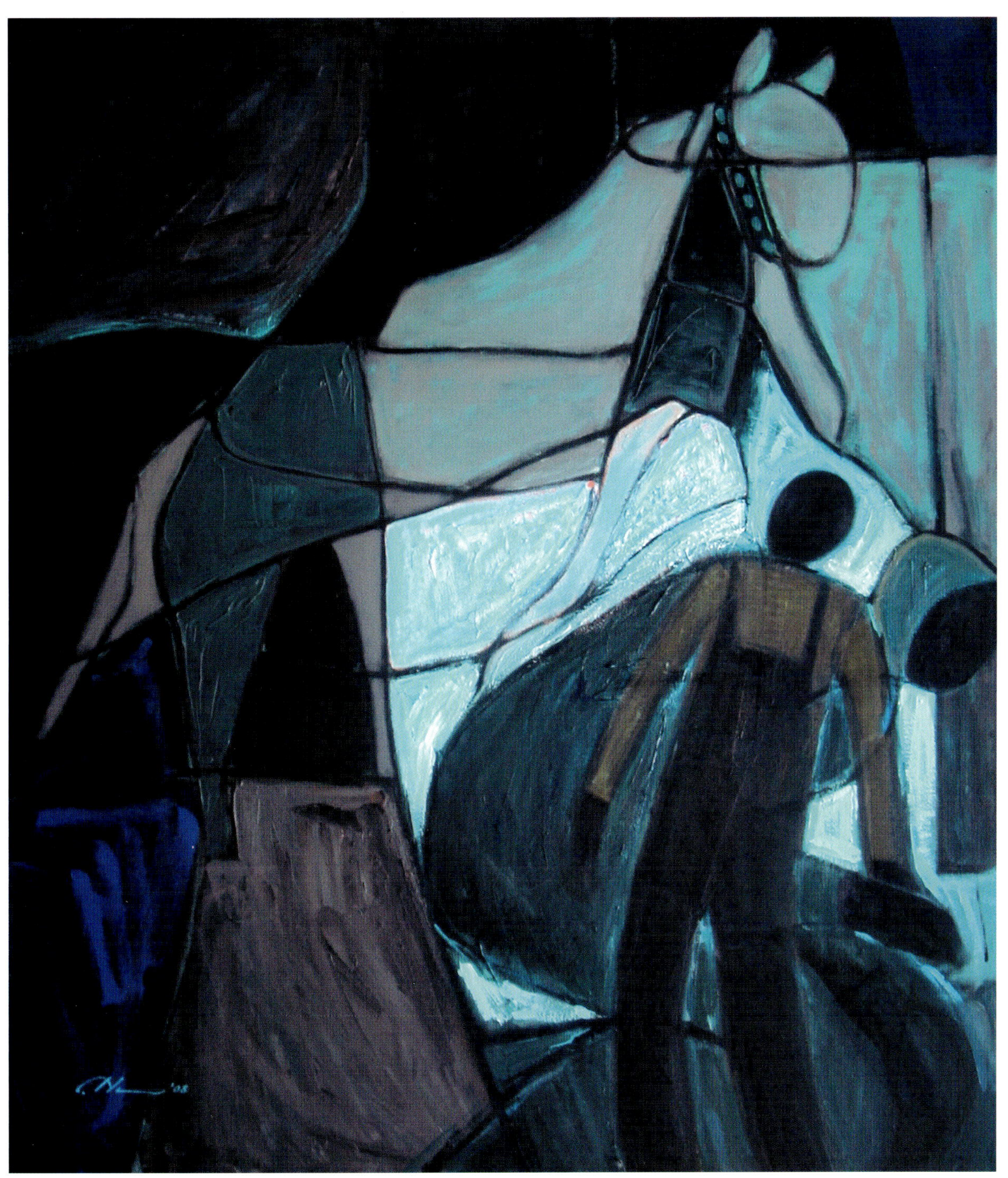

Spectre of the Hunt, 2008. Mixed media, 48 x 42 in.

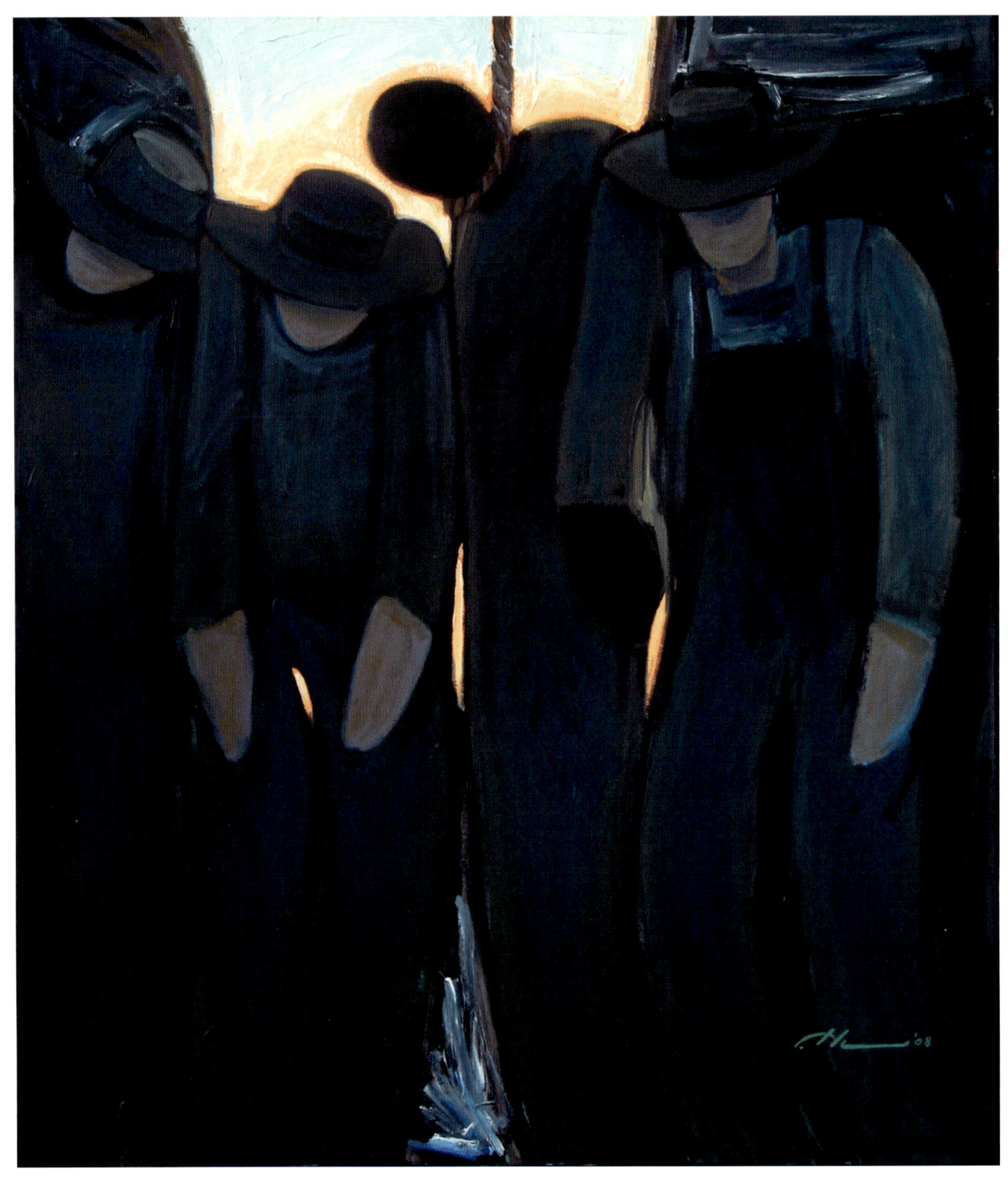

Property Loss, 2008. Acrylic on canvas, 48 x 42 in.

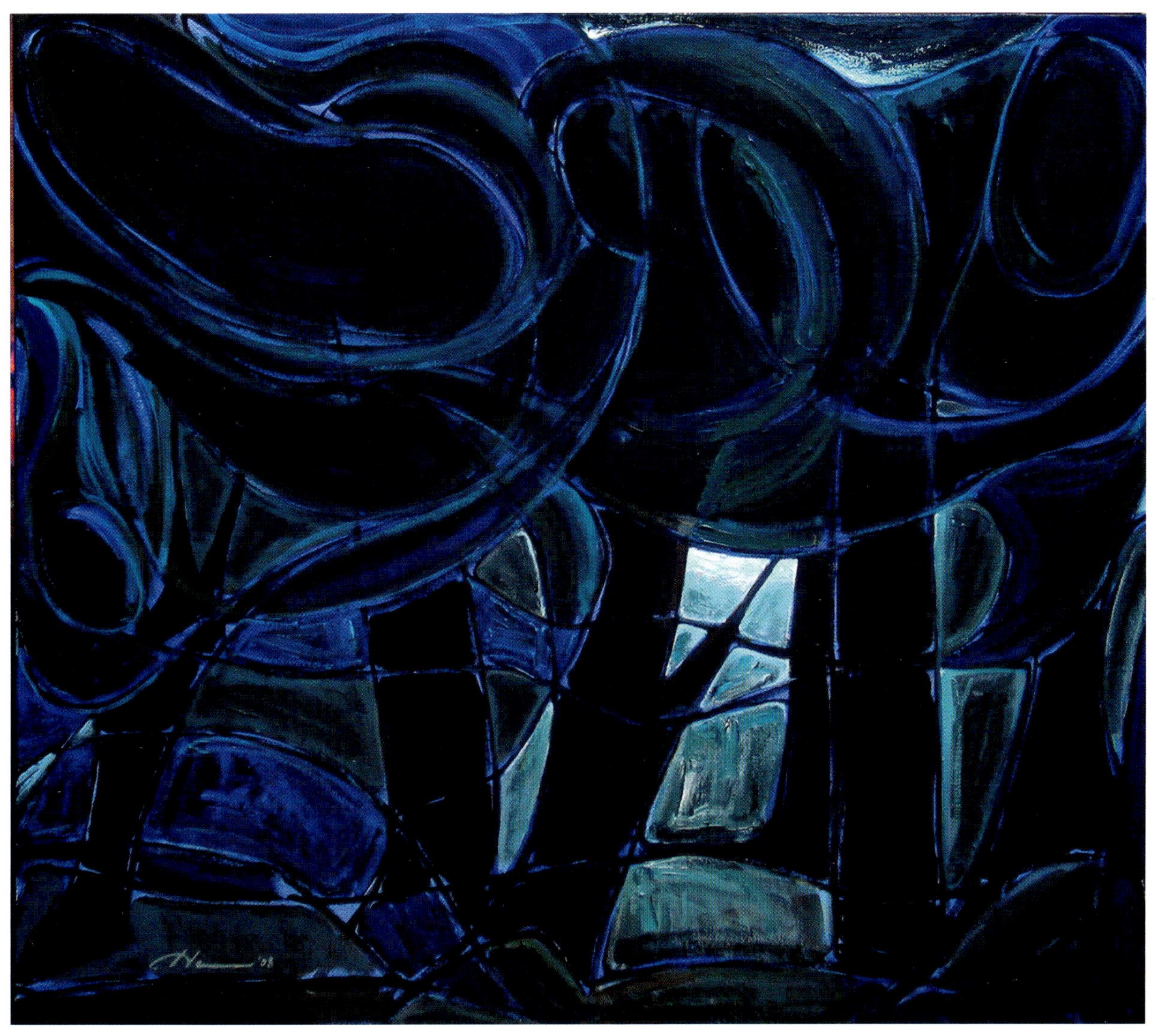

Promising Portal, 2008. Acrylic on canvas, 42 x 48 in.

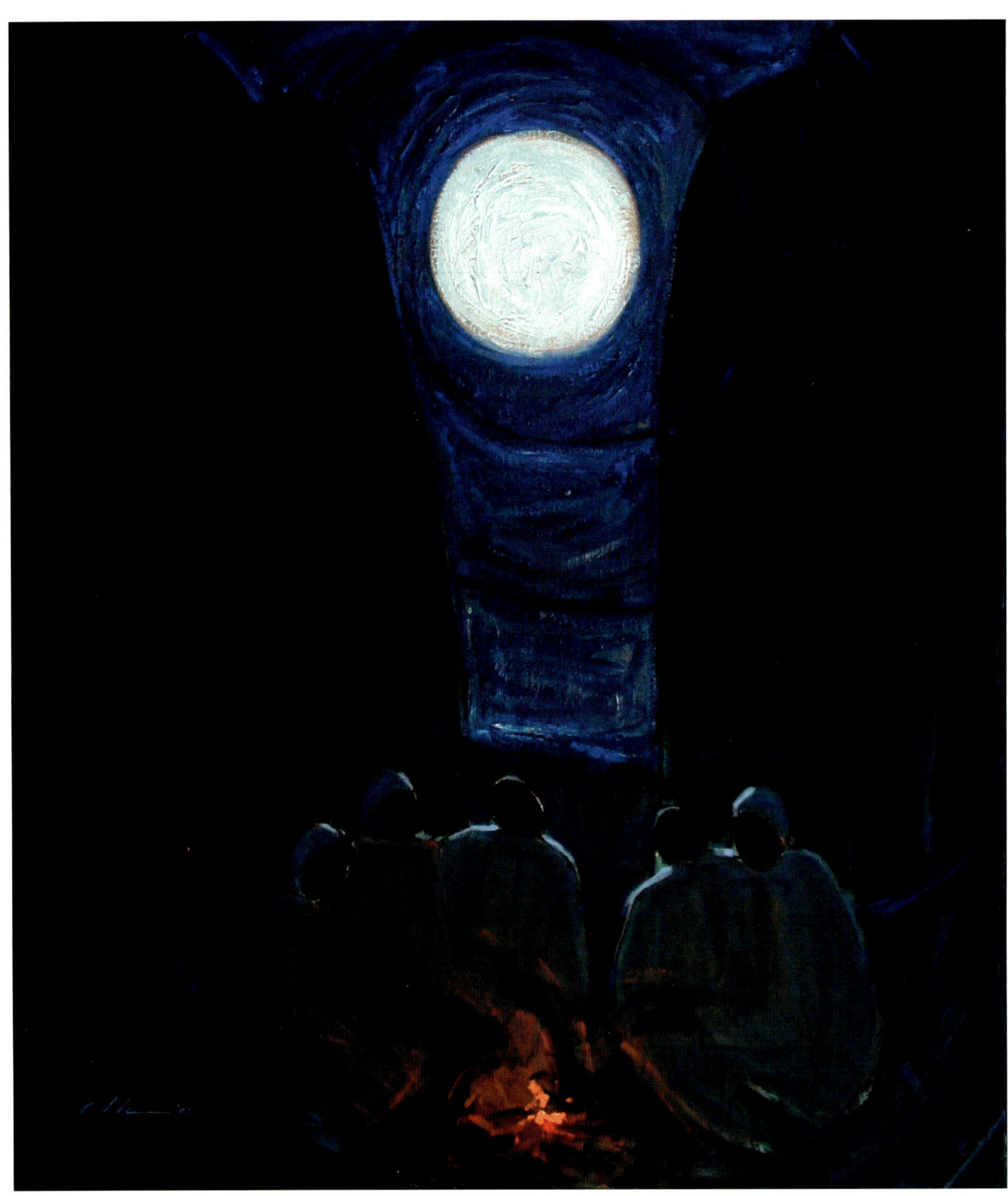

House of Refuge, 2008. Acrylic on canvas, 48 x 42 in.

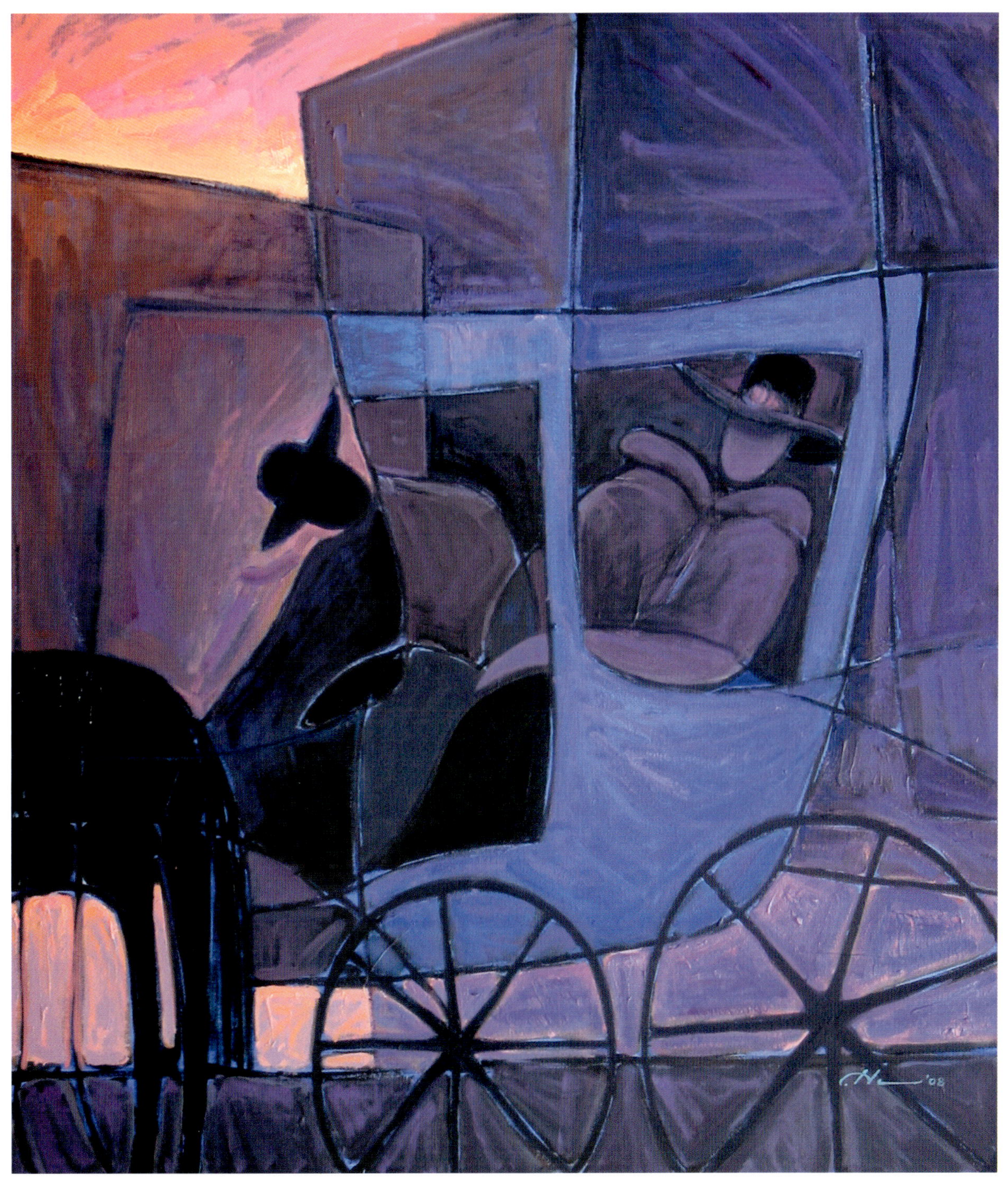

In Plain Sight, 2008. Acrylic on canvas, 48 x 42 in.

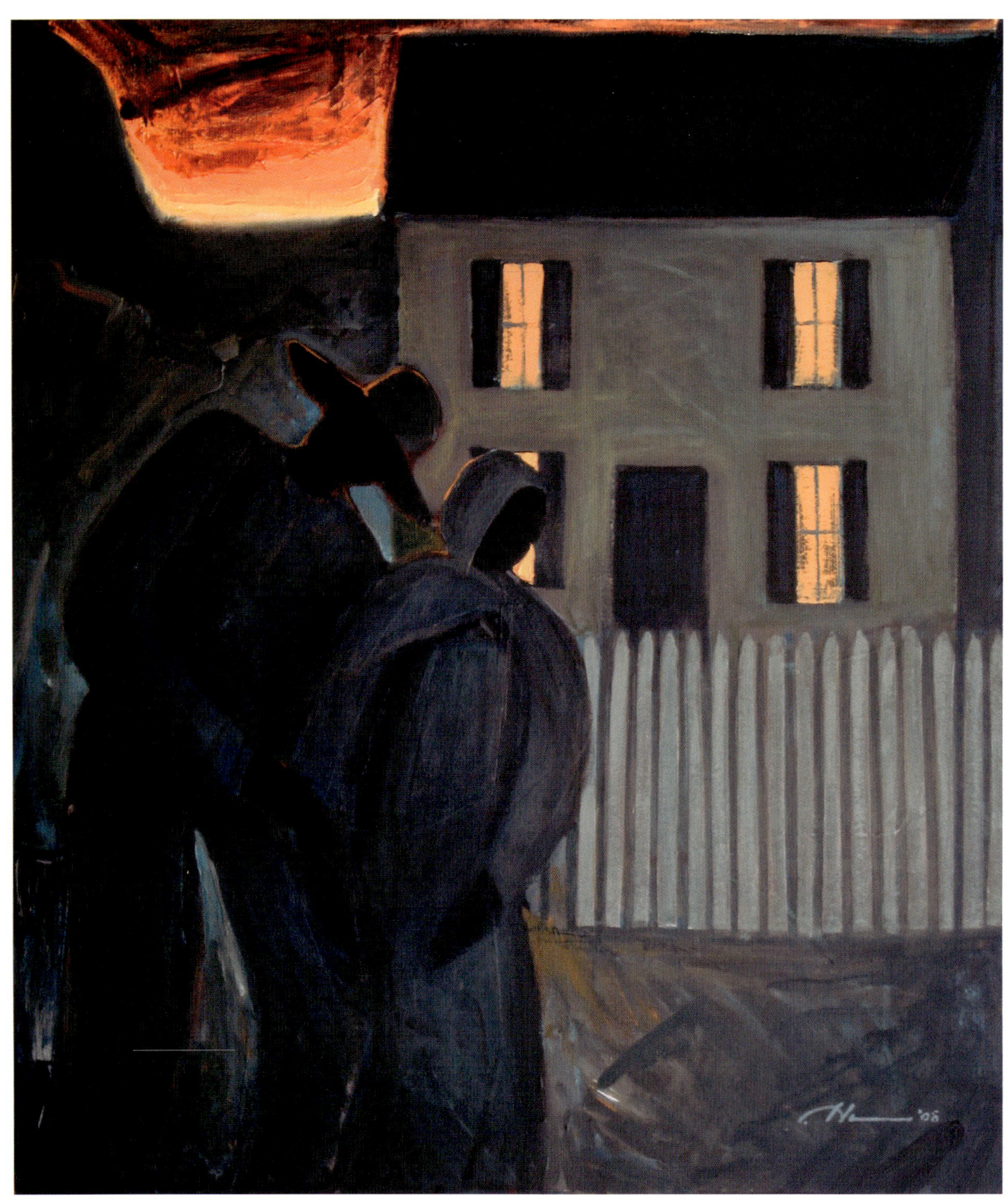

Freedom Stop, 2008. Mixed media, 48 x 42 in.

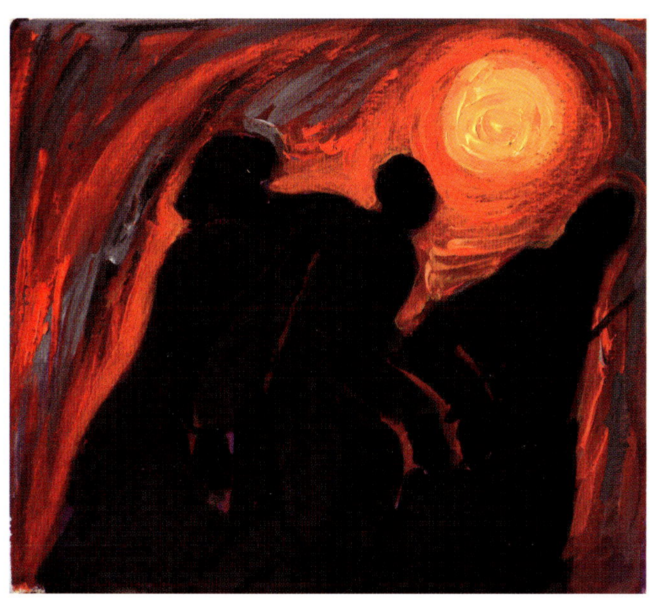

After Harriet (Study), 2008. Acrylic on paper, 6½ x 7 in.

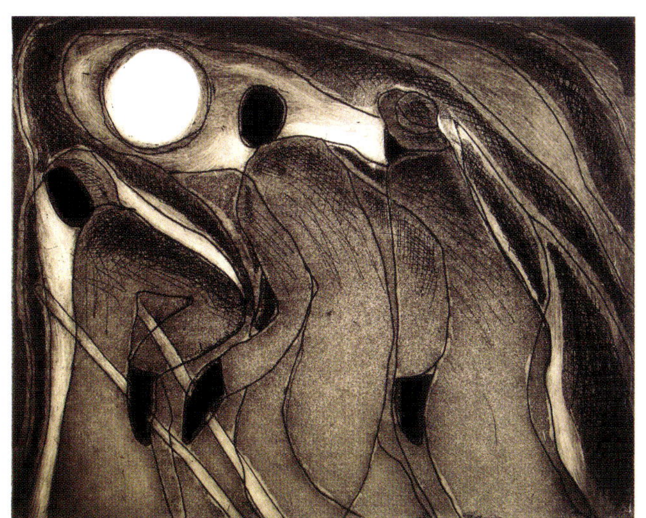

After Harriet, 2008. Etching, 11 x 14 in.

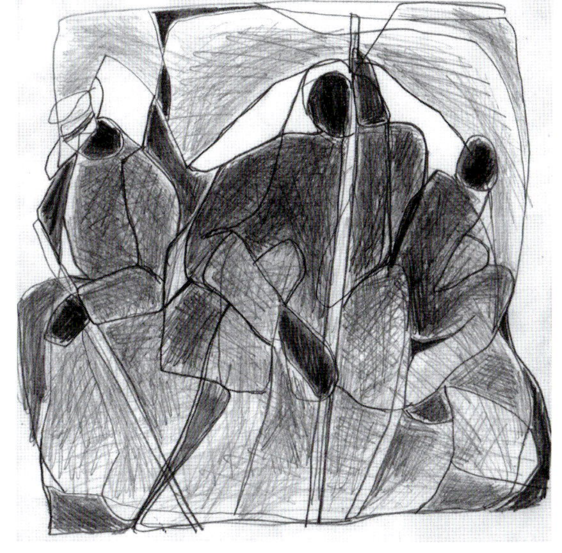

Dawn of Hope (Study), 2008. Pencil, 8¼ x 8¼ in.

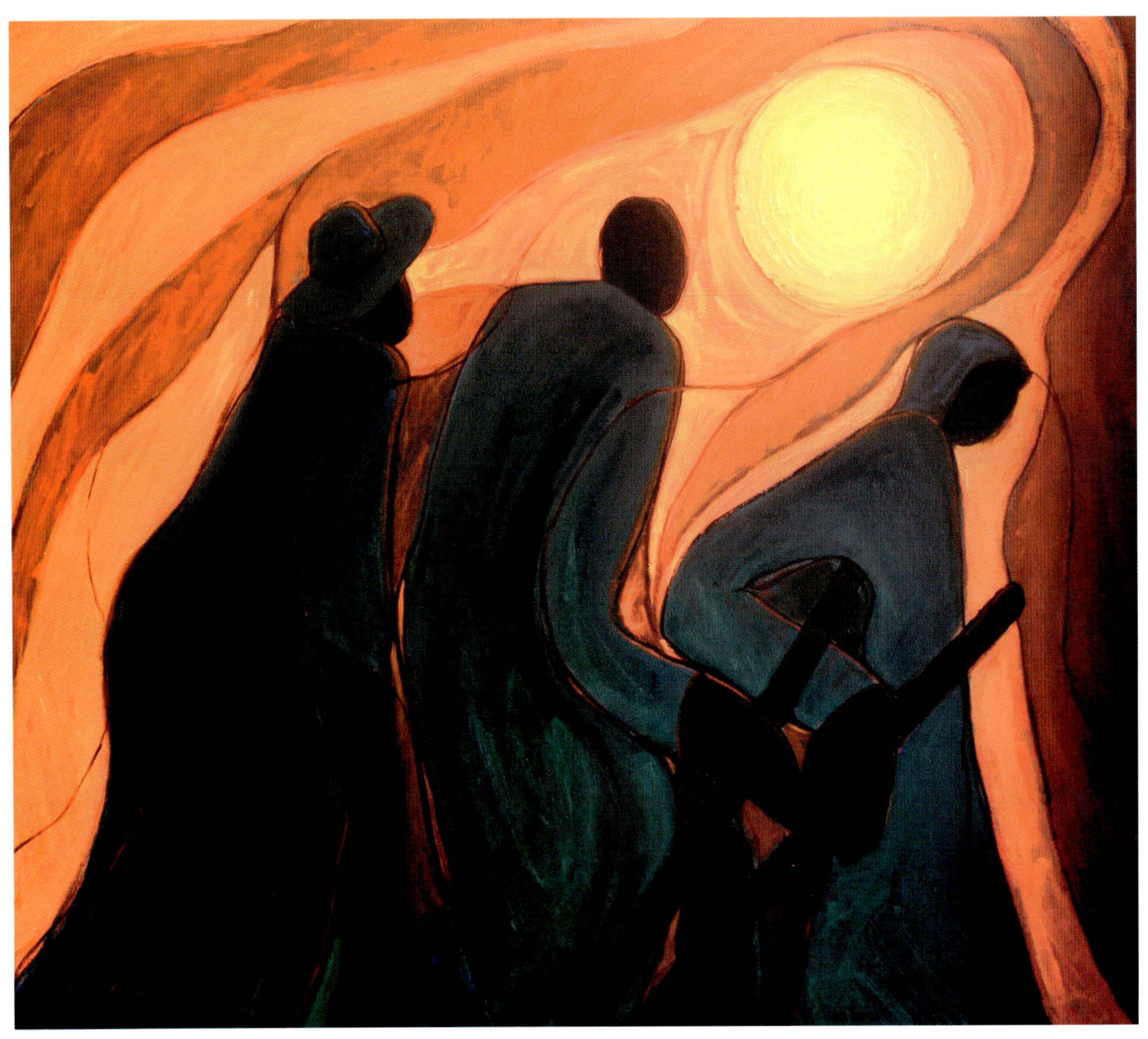

After Harriet, 2008. Mixed media, 42 x 48 in.

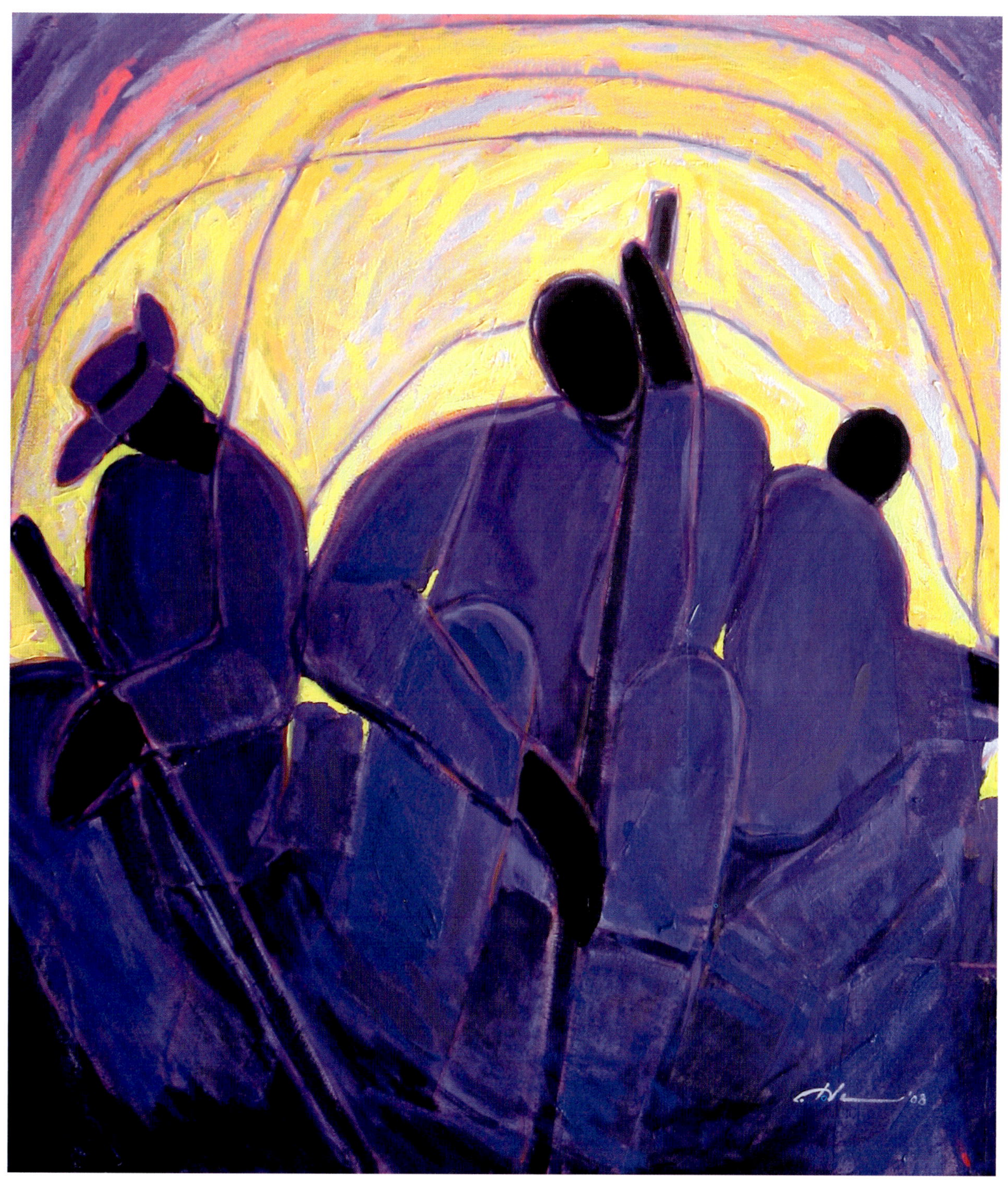

Dawn of Hope, 2008. Mixed media, 48 x 42 in.

THE FOURTH MOVEMENT: Color in Freedom

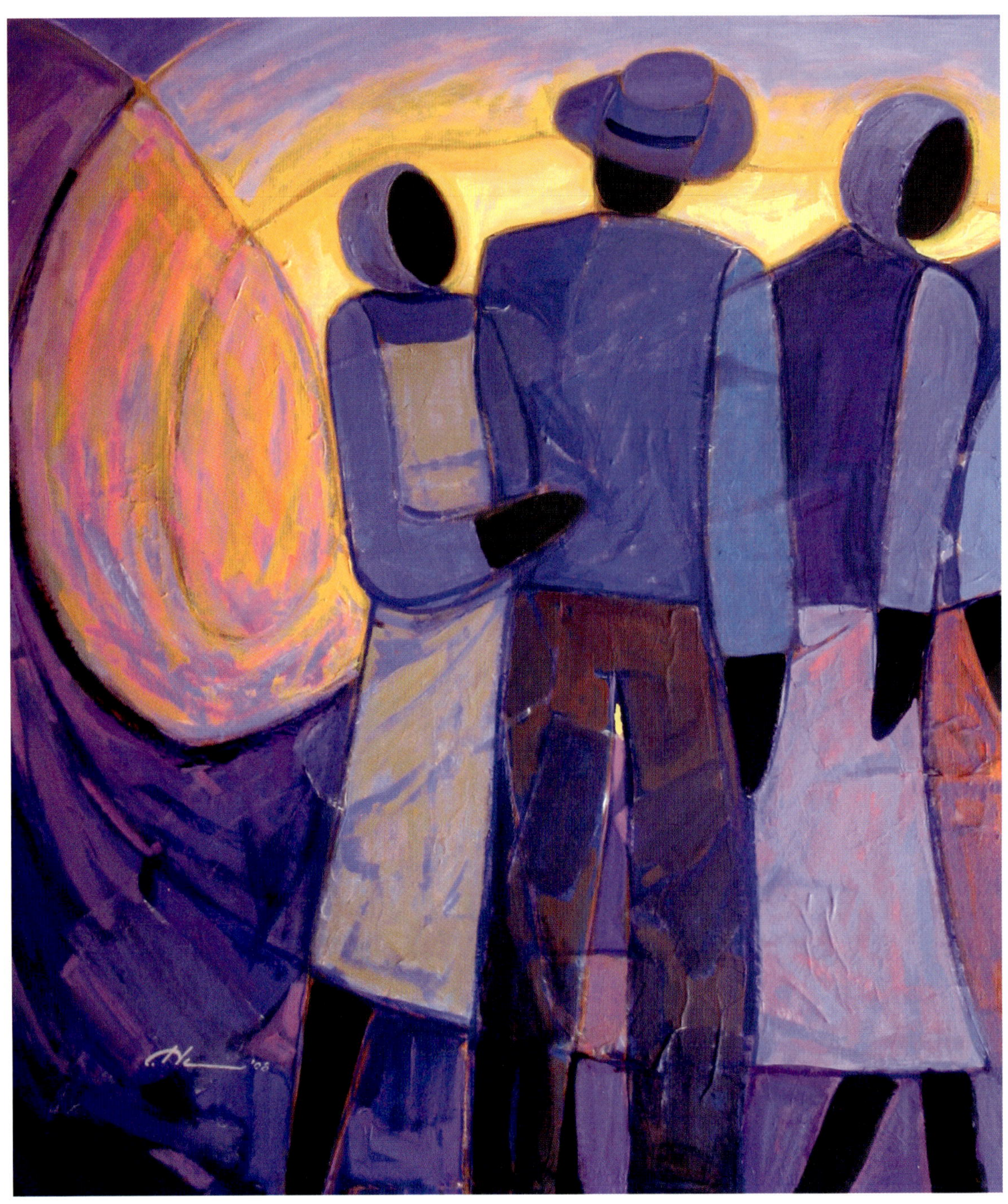

Freedom Realized (Diptych), 2008. Mixed media, 48 x 42 in. each

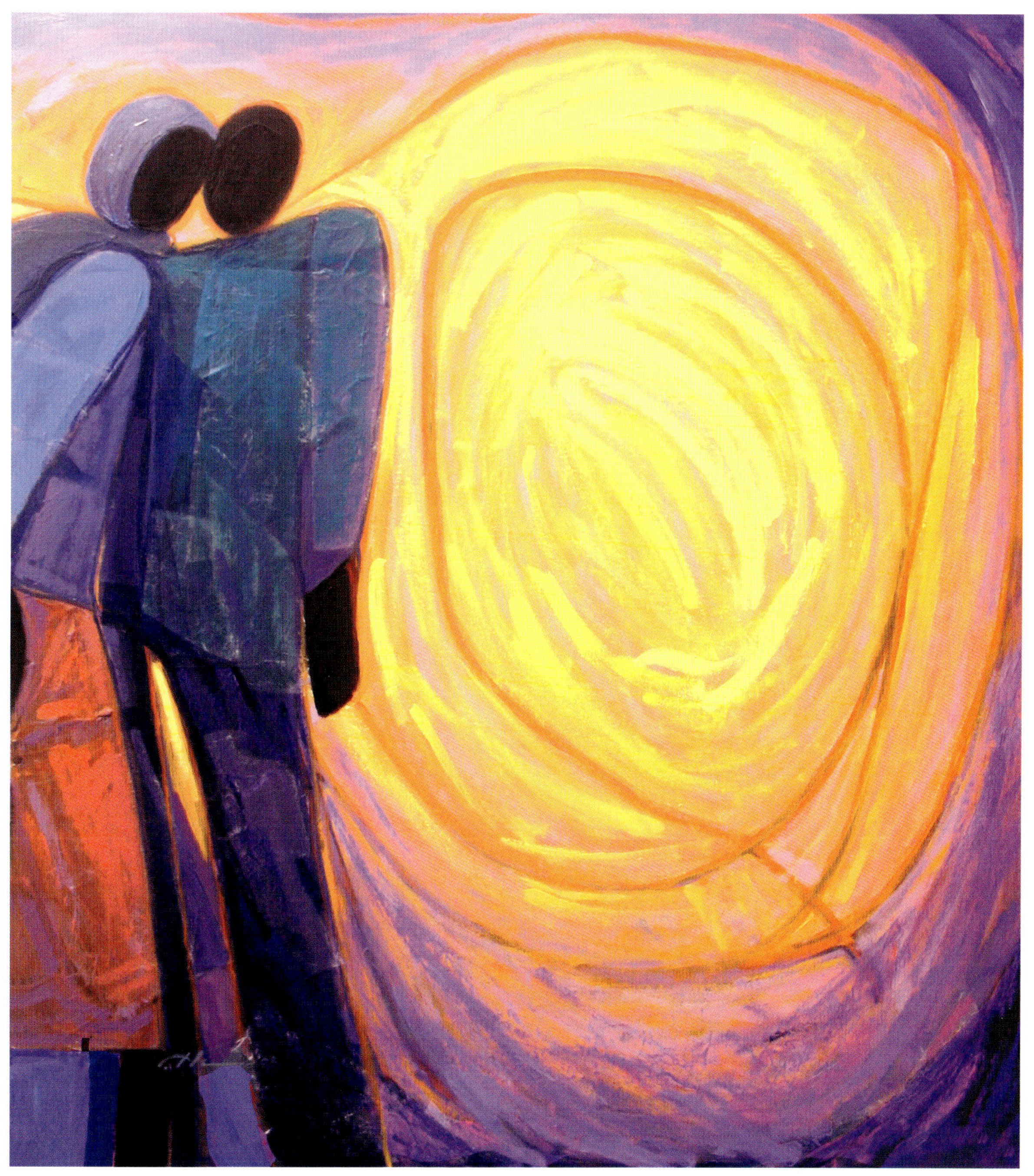

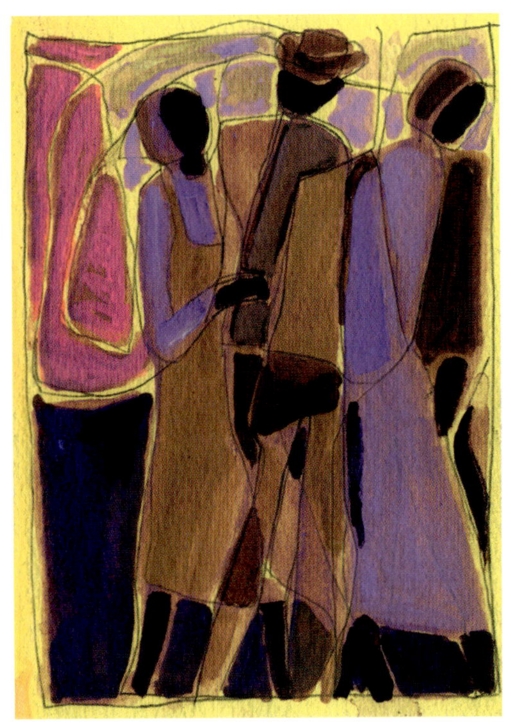

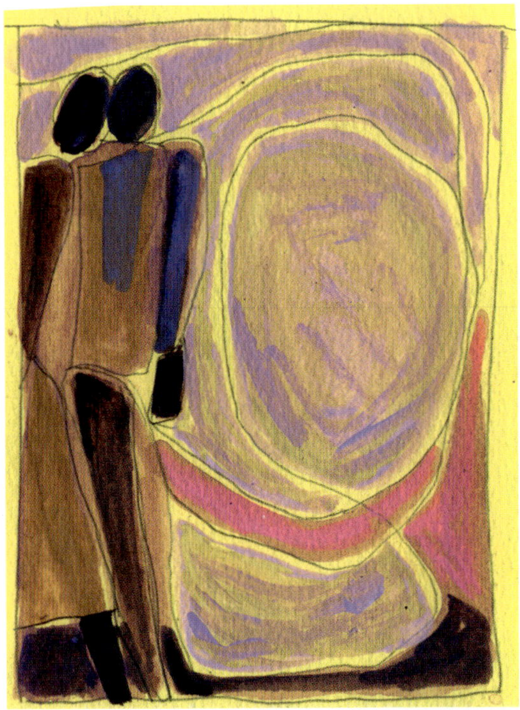

Freedom Realized (Study), 2008. Acrylic on paper, 6¼ x 9¼ in.

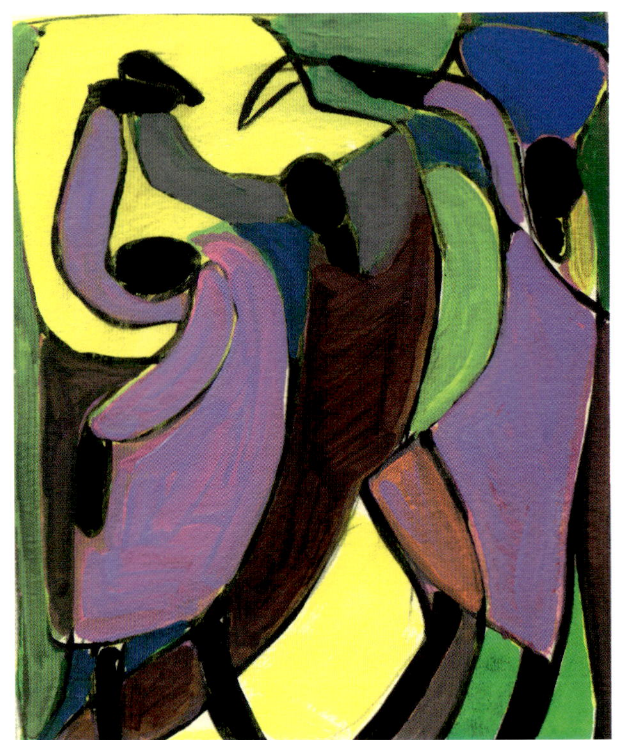

Jubilation (Study), 2008. Acrylic on paper, 8 x 7½ in.

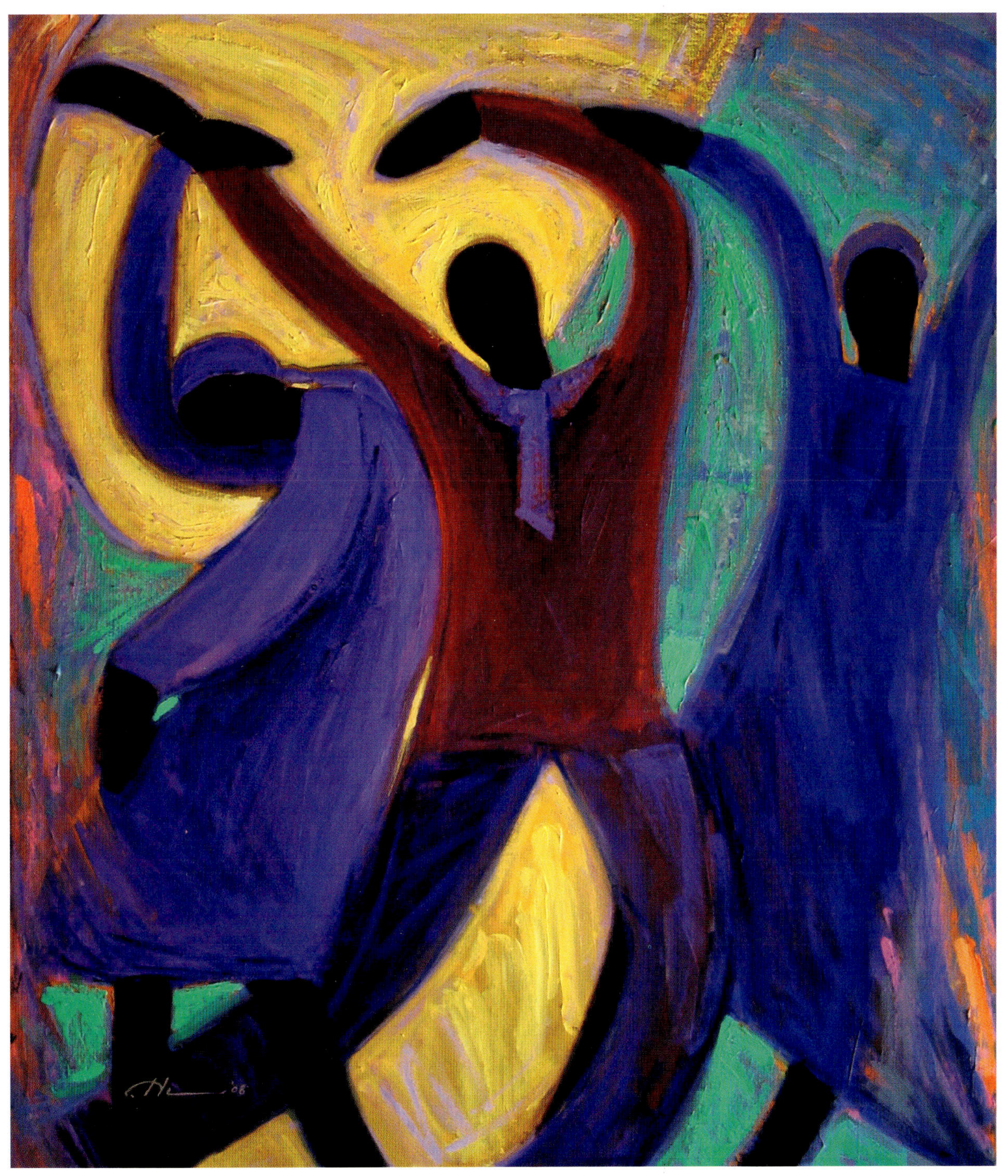

Jubilation, 2008. Mixed media, 48 x 42 in.

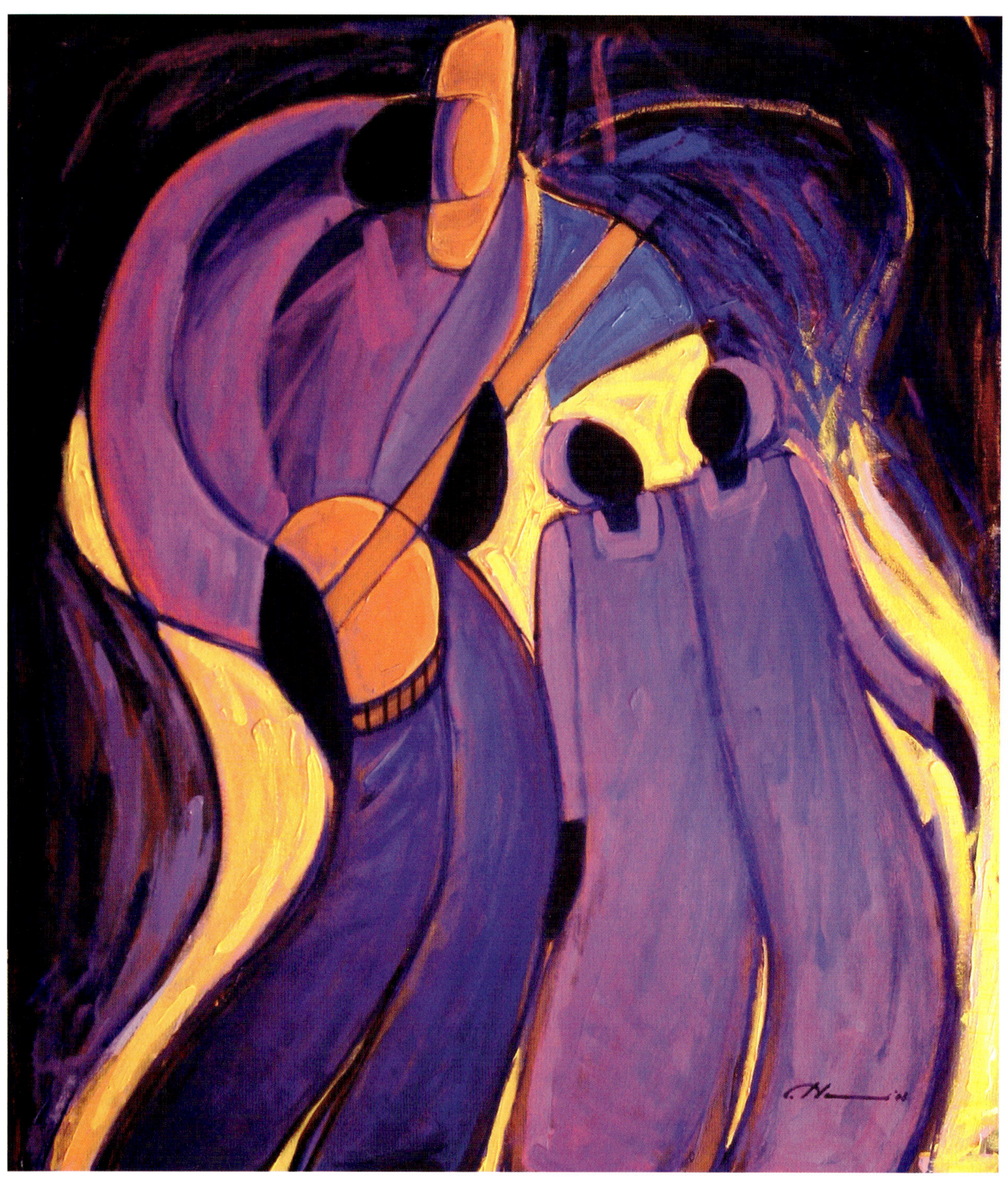

Rhythm of Renewal, 2008. Acrylic on canvas, 48 x 42 in.

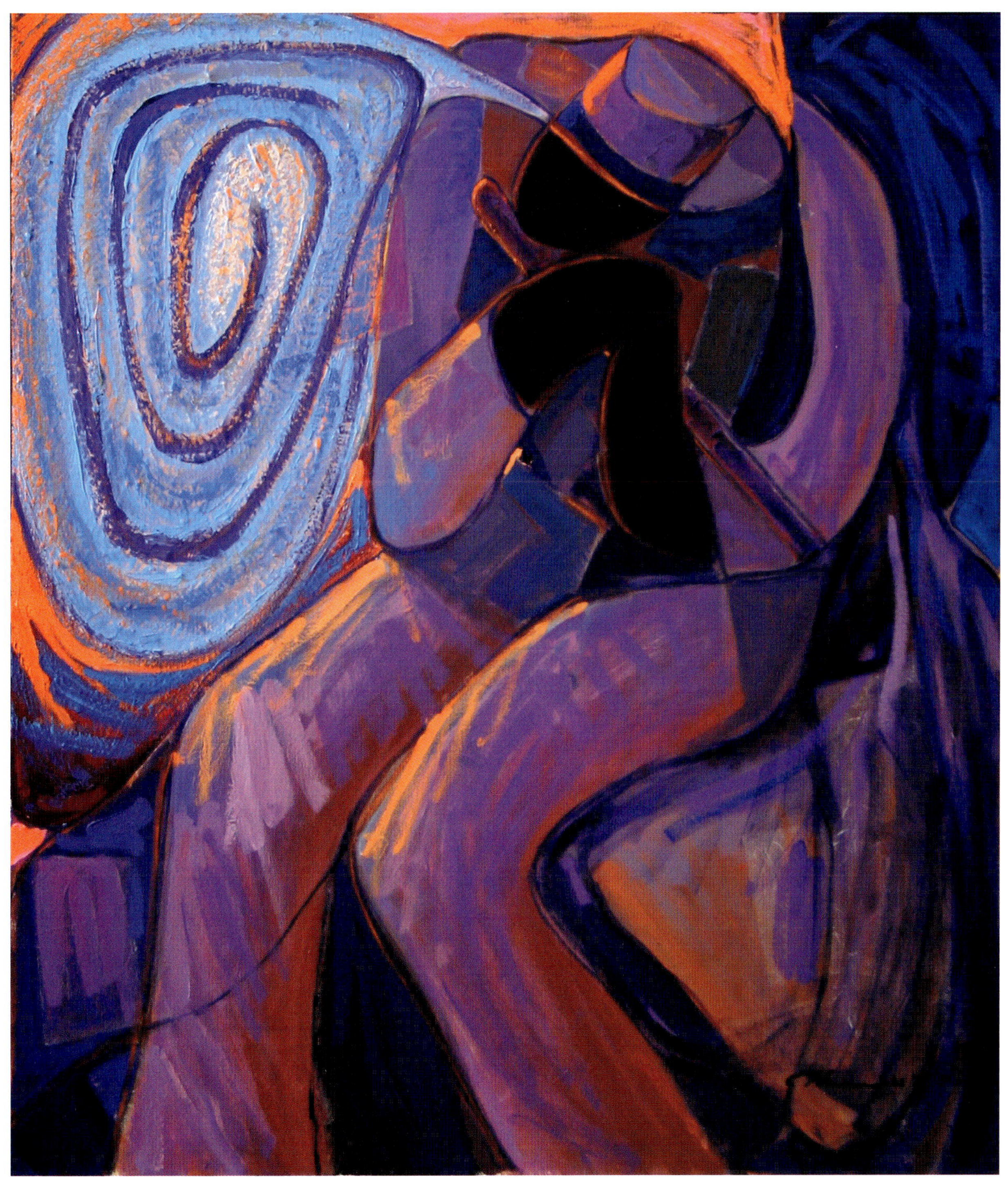

Magnificent Melody, 2008. Mixed media, 48 x 42 in.

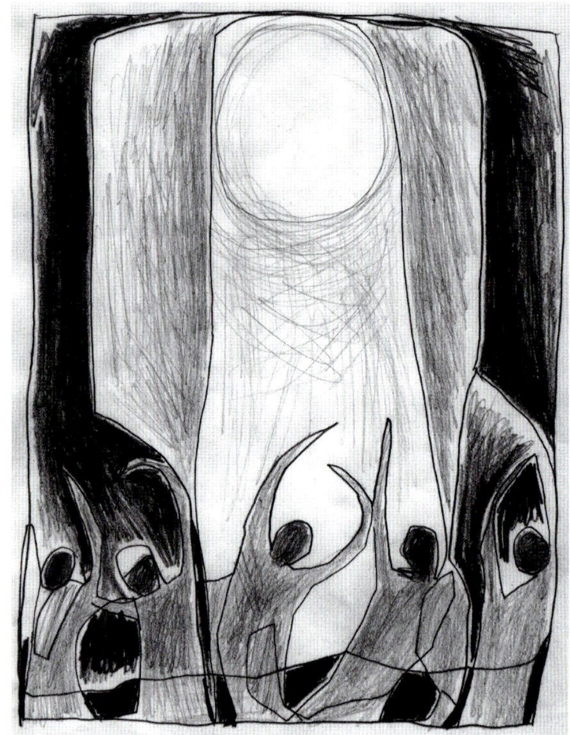

Righteous Rejoicing (Study), 2008. Pencil, 9½ x 7¼ in.

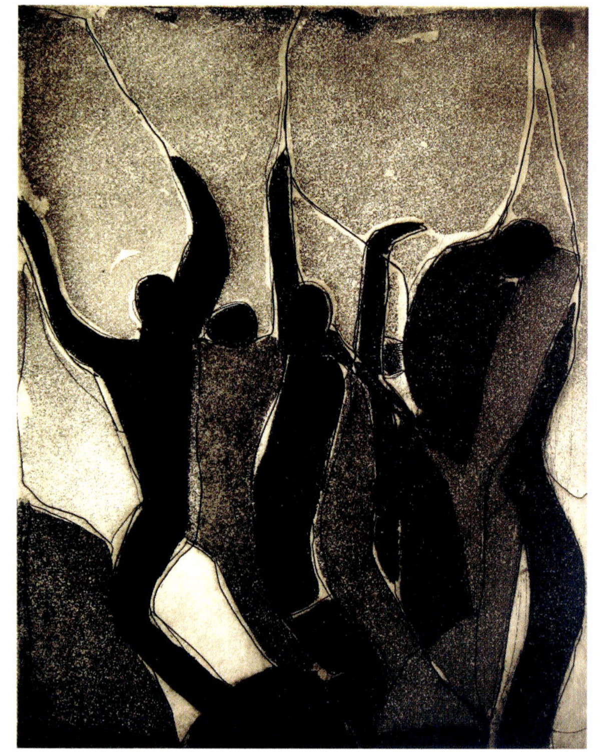

Righteous Rejoicing, 2008. Etching, 14 x 11 in.

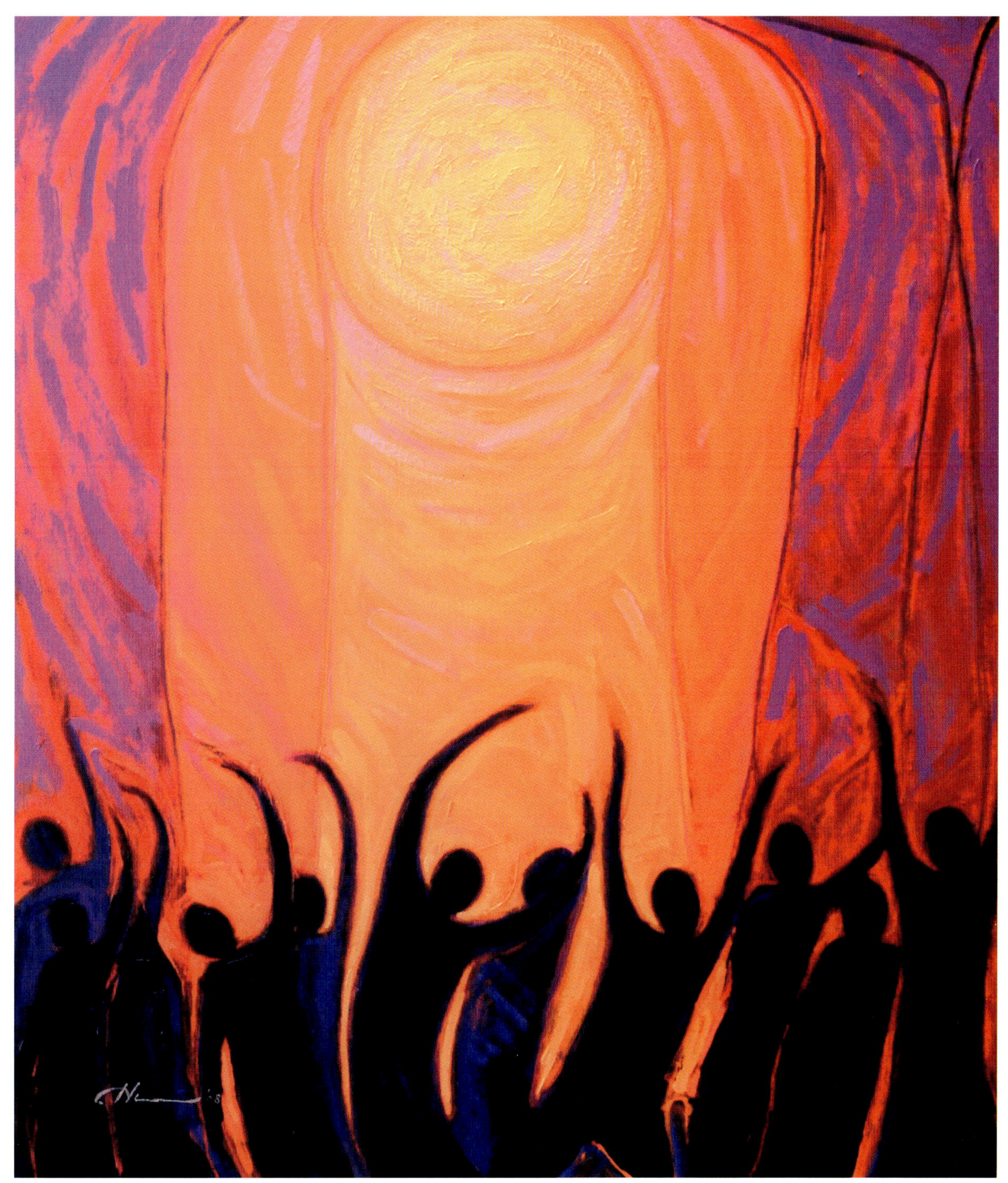

Righteous Rejoicing, 2008. Mixed media, 48 x 42 in.

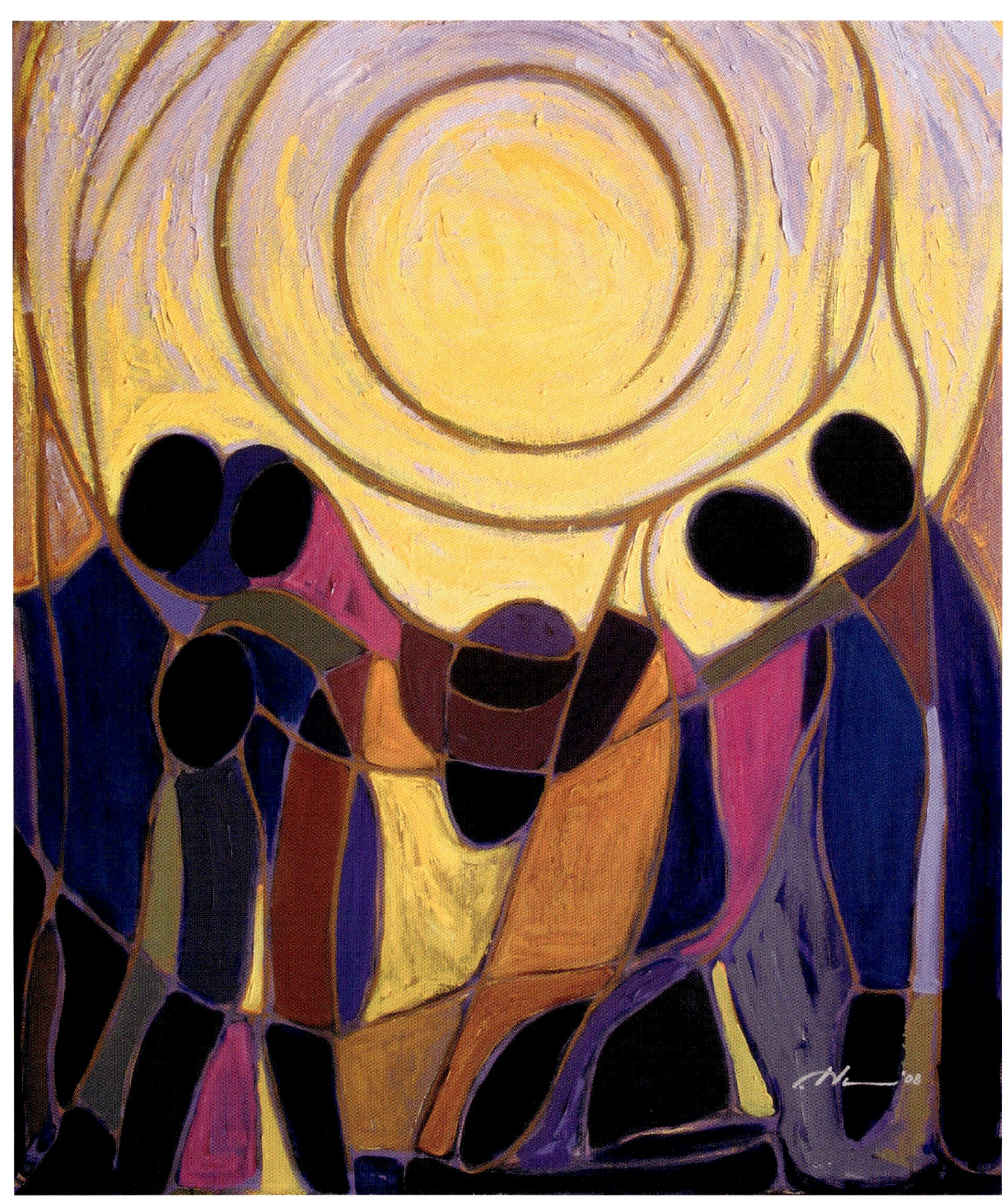

Sun Warms the Freemen, 2008. Mixed media, 48 x 42 in.

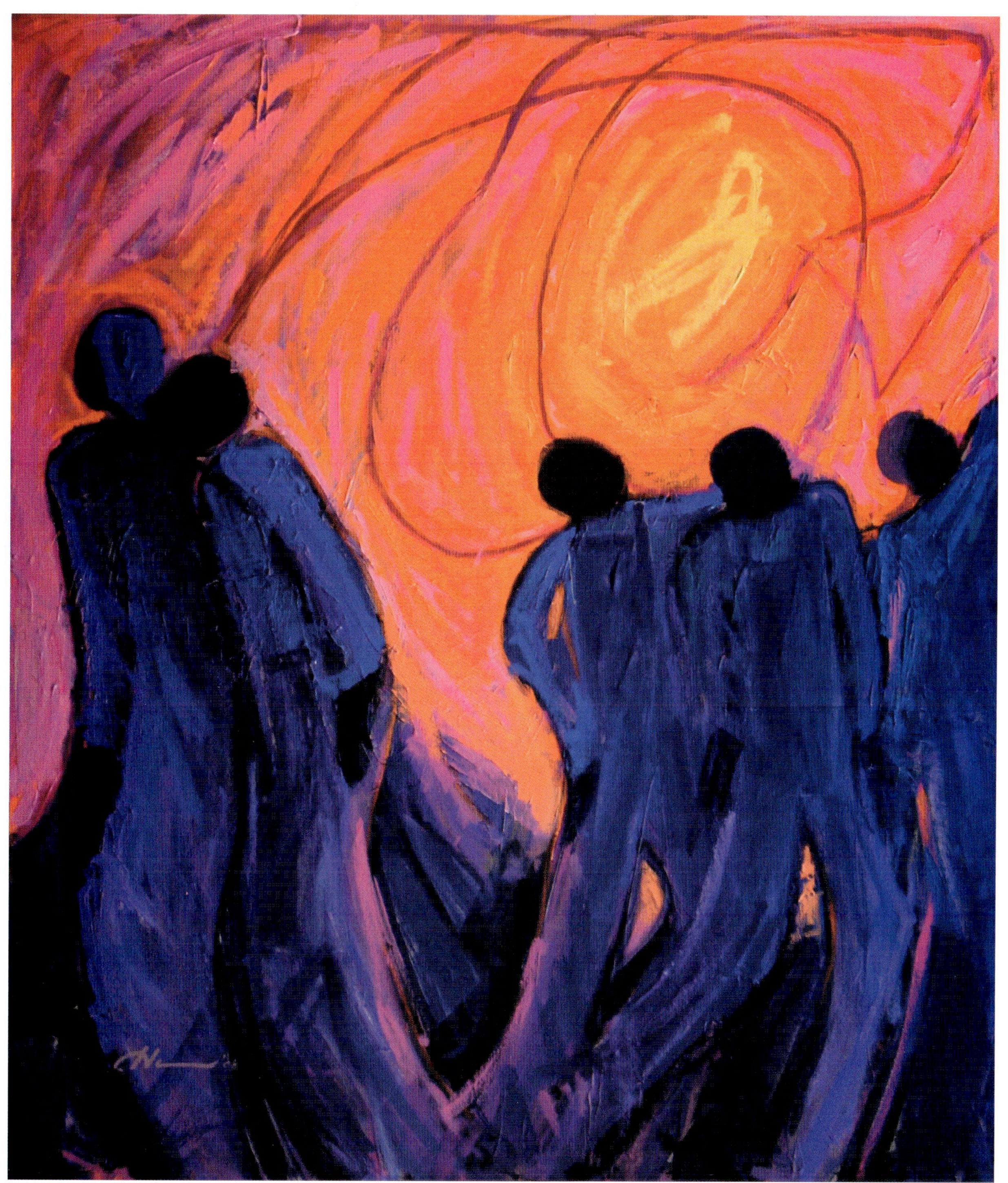

Responsibility of Freedom, 2008. Mixed media, 48 x 42 in.

Index of Artworks